101 LOW-FAT FEASTS
TRIED-AND-TESTED RECIPES

Hylas Publishing
Publisher: Sean Moore
Creative Director: Karen Prince
Designer: Gus Yoo
Editor: Beth Adelman

First Published in 2003 by *BBC Worldwide Ltd*,
Woodlands,

80 Wood Lane, London W12 0TT All photographs © BBC
Good Food Magazine 2003 and *BBC Vegetarian Good
Food Magazine* 2003

All the recipes contained in this book first appeared in
BBC Good Food Magazine and *BBC Vegetarian Good Food
Magazine*.

Published in the United States by
Hylas Publishing
129 Main Street, Irvington,
New York 10533

Copyright © BBC Worldwide 2002

The moral right of the author has been asserted.

Edited by Gilly Cubitt
Commissioning Editor: Vivien Bowler
Project Editors: Rebecca Hardie and Sarah Miles
Designers: Kathryn Gammon and Annette Peppis
Design Manager: Sarah Ponder
Production Controller: Christopher Tinker

First American Edition published in 2003
02 03 04 05 10 9 8 7 6 5 4 3 2 1

ISBN 1-59258-021-1

Set in Helvetica and ITC Officina Sans

Printed and bound in Italy by LEGO SpA

Color origination by Radstock Reproductions Ltd,
Midsomer Norton

Distributed by St. Martin's Press

101 LOW-FAT FEASTS
TRIED AND TESTED RECIPES

Editor-in-chief
Orlando Murrin

Contents

Introduction

Yes, it's possible! Low-fat recipes that don't cut corners on flavor or satisfaction. And this is no one-dish wonder—you'll find more than 100 *BBC Good Food Magazine* recipes in this book to help keep you trim.

We've revamped everyday dishes, so you don't need to cut out your favorite meals, and we've introduced new and exciting recipes, like the *Chicken Skewers with Cucumber Dip* pictured opposite (see page 104 for the recipe), to expand your repertoire. After all, when you're trying to eat less, it's important to make what you do have as delicious and tempting as possible.

Each recipe comes with a nutritional breakdown, so you can check not only calories and fat content, but also the amount of saturated and unsaturated fats, which is crucial for those who

are watching their cholesterol levels.

Our recipes have all been tried and tested in the Good Food kitchen, so we can guarantee fabulous results every time. This is lean cuisine with loads of flavors, no-fuss preparation and certainly no guilt. Use these recipes regularly and you will soon see the results you've been waiting for.

Editor, *BBC Good Food Magazine*

Orlando Murrin

Conversion tables

NOTES ON THE RECIPES
• Eggs are large, unless stated otherwise.
• Wash all fresh produce before preparation.

OVEN TEMPERATURES

°F	°C	Gas	Fan °C	Oven temp.
225	110	¼	90	Very cool
250	120	½	100	Very cool
275	140	1	120	Cool or slow
300	150	2	130	Cool or slow
325	160	3	140	Warm
350	180	4	160	Moderate
375	190	5	170	Moderately hot
400	200	6	180	Fairly hot
425	220	7	200	Hot
450	230	8	210	Very hot
475	240	9	220	Very hot

APPROXIMATE WEIGHT CONVERSIONS
• All the recipes in this book use American measurements. The charts on this page and the next will help you convert to metric measurements. Conversions are approximate and have been rounded up or down. Follow one set of measurements only; do not mix the two.
• Cup measurements have not been listed here, because they vary from ingredient to ingredient. Please use a kitchen scale to weigh dry/solid ingredients.
• Where a recipe calls for a can of something (for example, tuna or tomatoes), we have listed what is generally a standard size can. If the standard cans in your area are a slightly different size, a small difference should not affect the outcome of the recipe.

SPOON MEASURES

• Spoon measurements are level unless otherwise specified.
• 1 teaspoon = 5ml
• 1 tablespoon = 15ml
• 1 Australian tablespoon = 20ml (cooks in Australia should measure 3 teaspoons where 1 tablespoon is specified in a recipe)

APPROXIMATE LIQUID CONVERSIONS

US	Metric	Imperial	Australia
¼ cup	50ml	2fl oz	¼ cup
½ cup	125ml	4fl oz	½ cup
¾ cup	175ml	6fl oz	¾ cup
1 cup	225ml	8fl oz	1 cup
1¼ cups	300ml	10fl oz/½ pint	½ pint
2 cups/1 pint	450ml	16fl oz	2 cups
2½ cups	600ml	20fl oz/1 pint	1 pint
1 quart	1 litre	35fl oz/1¾ pints	1¾ pints

Try this soup, cooked only to the end of step one,
as a sauce for freshly cooked pasta.

Roasted Tomato Soup

1 large onion, chopped
2 tbsp olive oil
1–2 garlic cloves
2lb tomatoes, chopped
1 red pepper, seeded and chopped
4 carrots, chopped
salt & pepper to taste
2 cups vegetable stock
crusty bread, to serve

Takes 50 minutes • Serves 4

1 Preheat the oven to 400°F. Toss together the onion, oil, garlic, tomatoes, pepper and carrots in a large roasting pan. Season with plenty of salt and freshly ground black pepper and roast for 40 minutes.
2 Pour in the stock and stir, scraping the bottom of the pan to release the scorched vegetable juices.
3 Transfer to a food processor and process until smooth. Put back in the pan and gently reheat. Adjust the seasoning to taste and serve with toasted crusty bread.

• Per serving: 155 calories, protein 4g, carbohydrate 21g, fat 7g, saturated fat 1g, fiber 6g, added sugar none, salt 0.61g

Use a green-leaf lettuce, for the best color.

Time step two carefully or the green freshness will be lost.

Lettuce Soup

1oz butter
1 onion, chopped
2 medium potatoes,
peeled and chopped
1 garlic clove
16fl oz vegetable stock
salt & pepper to taste
2 fresh heads of lettuce, finely sliced
8fl oz milk
a pinch of nutmeg
heavy cream and snipped chives,
to serve

Takes 40 minutes • Serves 8

1 Melt the butter in a large pot with a lid, then stir in the onion, potatoes and garlic. Add the stock, season with salt and pepper, and simmer for 20 minutes, covered, until the potatoes are tender.

2 Add the lettuce and cook, covered, for 3–4 minutes until the stock returns to a boil and the lettuce is semi-wilted.

3 Puree in a blender or with a handheld electric mixer, then return to the pot. Add the milk. Season, add a pinch of nutmeg and serve with a swirl of cream and a sprinkling of chives.

• Per serving: 71 calories, protein 2g, carbohydrate 7g, fat 4g, saturated fat 2g, fiber 1g, added sugar none, salt 0.3g

To make deep-fried sage leaves, drop clean dry leaves into deep hot oil for a few seconds, until they are crisp but still green.

Cream of Pumpkin Soup

3lb pumpkin, peeled, sliced and seeded
3 tbsp olive oil
1 large onion, chopped
2 garlic cloves, chopped
2 tsp cumin seeds
1 potato, peeled and chopped
6 fresh thyme sprigs or 1 tsp dried
2½ cups vegetable stock
salt & pepper to taste
cream or plain yogurt, to serve
deep-fried sage leaves, to garnish

Takes 45 minutes • Serves 6

1 Cut the pumpkin into chunks. Heat the oil in a large pan, then saute the onion, garlic and cumin for 2–3 minutes. Add the pumpkin and potato and cook, stirring, for 5–6 minutes. Add the leaves from the thyme sprigs (or use dried) to the pan.

2 Pour in the stock and simmer for about 15 minutes until the pumpkin and potato are soft. puree in a blender until smooth, then pour into a pot, heat through and season with salt and pepper.

3 Serve each portion with cream, lightly stirred in. Garnish with fried sage leaves.

• Per serving: 122 calories, protein 2g, carbohydrate 11g, fat 8g, saturated fat 1g, fiber 2g, added sugar none, salt 0.4g

This is a mildly spiced soup, perfect for chilly evenings.
Reheat leftovers for lunch the next day.

Sweet Potato and Lentil Soup

4oz red lentils
(no need to soak)
1 onion, chopped
a knob of butter
1 garlic clove, finely chopped
2 tbsp curry paste
1lb sweet potatoes,
peeled and cubed
1lb starchy potatoes,
peeled and cubed
4 cups hot vegetable stock
salt & pepper to taste
2 tbsp chopped fresh mint (optional)
5oz plain yogurt
crusty bread or pita, to serve

Takes 40 minutes • Serves 4

1 Cook the lentils in boiling water for 15 minutes. Cook the onion in the butter for 8 minutes until softened and beginning to brown. Stir in the garlic, curry paste and potatoes. Cook for 5 minutes, stirring.

2 Drain the lentils. Add to the potatoes with the stock and cook for 12–15 minutes until the potatoes are fully cooked. Puree in a blender until smooth. Return to the pan, season with salt and pepper and heat through.

3 Stir the mint, if using, into the yogurt and season. Ladle the soup into bowls and swirl in the yogurt. Serve with bread.

• Per serving: 330 calories, protein 14g, carbohydrate 63g, fat 4g, saturated fat 1g, fiber 6g, added sugar none, salt 1.53kg

Choose the least knobbly Jerusalem artichokes
you can find, to make peeling easier.

Jerusalem Artichoke Soup

1oz butter
2 onions, sliced
1lb 2oz Jerusalem artichokes
2 cups vegetable stock
(or the water in which you
have boiled the potatoes)
salt & white pepper to taste
a pinch of sugar
2 cups milk
a knob of butter or 2 tbsp cream,
to finish
croutons, to serve

Takes 1¼ hours • Serves 8

1 Heat the butter in a large pot. Add the onions,
cover and let them sweat for 5 minutes until soft but
not brown. Peel and slice the Jerusalem artichokes,
add to the onions and sweat for 15
minutes or until just tender.
2 Pour in the stock or potato water, and season
with salt, white pepper and the sugar. Simmer for 20
minutes until soft.
3 Puree in batches, then pour back into the pot
along with the milk. Bring to a boil, then stir in the
butter or cream. Serve with croutons.

• Per serving: 179 calories, protein 5g, carbohydrate 19g, fat
10g, saturated fat 6g, fiber 3g, added sugar trace, salt 0.61g

A glorious clear pink soup with matchstick vegetables.

Add a spoonful of sour cream to serve.

Chunky Beet Soup

2 large, raw beets peeled
2 large carrots, peeled
2 celery stalks
2 garlic cloves
4 large tomatoes, skinned
2oz butter
1 large onion, thinly sliced
6 cups vegetable stock
salt & pepper to taste
sprig of parsley, 1 bay leaf and
2 whole cloves, tied in muslin
5 oz sour cream, to serve

Takes 2 hours • Serves 8

1 Cut the beets, carrots and celery into thick matchsticks. Crush the garlic and chop the tomatoes. Heat the butter in a large pot and add the onion, beets, carrots and celery.

2 Cook gently for 10 minutes over low heat, stirring occasionally. Add the garlic and tomatoes and continue to cook for another 5 minutes. Pour in the stock, season well with salt and pepper and add the herbs and spices tied in muslin. Cover and simmer for 1½ hours.

3 When the time is up, remove the muslin bag and check the soup for seasoning. Serve in bowls with a dollop of sour cream on top.

• Per serving: 89 calories, protein 2g, carbohydrate 8g, fat 6g, saturated fat 3g, fiber 2g, added sugar none, salt 0.89g

A simple soup that allows the flavor of
fresh summer vegetables to shine through.

Vegetable and Pesto Soup

1 tbsp olive oil
1 onion, chopped
8oz new potatoes, sliced
2 vegetable stock cubes
4oz green beans, sliced
1lb zucchini, halved then sliced
salt & pepper to taste
2–3 tbsp pesto

Takes 30 minutes • Serves 4

1 Heat the oil in a large pot and saute the onion for 8 minutes until golden. Add the potato slices and mix well. Dissolve the stock cubes in 4 cups boiling water, then add to the pot. Bring to a boil and simmer for 7 minutes until the potatoes are just cooked.
2 Add the green beans to the pot and continue to cook for 5 minutes, adding the zucchini for the last 2 minutes of cooking time.
3 Season with plenty of salt and pepper. Remove from the heat and stir in 2 tablespoons of the pesto. Taste and add more pesto, if necessary. Serve hot.

• Per serving: 159 calories, protein 5g, carbohydrate 14g, fat 10g, saturated fat 2g, fiber 3g, added sugar none, salt 1.54g

Vary the combination of vegetables to suit yourself; even a bag of prepared stir-fry vegetables from the supermarket would do.

Asian Vegetable Broth

1 stalk lemongrass, thinly sliced
1in piece fresh ginger, sliced
2 garlic cloves, sliced
4 tbsp soy sauce
2 tbsp sake or dry sherry
finely grated zest and juice of 1 lime
1 tsp fine sugar
2 tbsp vegetable oil
2 carrots, cut into matchsticks
4oz baby corn, halved
1 large red chili, sliced
4oz oyster mushrooms, sliced
2oz baby spinach leaves
3oz beansprouts

Takes 20 minutes • Serves 4

1 Place the lemongrass, ginger and garlic in a large pot with the soy sauce, sake or sherry, lime zest and juice and caster sugar. Add 3 cups water and bring to a boil. Cover and simmer for 10 minutes. Strain and keep the broth warm.
2 Heat the oil in a large frying pan or wok, add the carrots, corn and chili and stir-fry for 2 minutes. Add the mushrooms, spinach and beansprouts and remove from the heat.
3 Divide the vegetables among four serving bowls, pour in the hot broth and serve immediately.

• Per serving: 130 calories, protein 4g, carbohydrate 9g, fat 8g, saturated fat 1g, fiber 3g, added sugar 1g, salt 2.3g

Look for fresh Japanese udon or yakisoba
noodles in the ethnic section of the supermarket.

Meal-in-a-bowl Noodle Soup

1 tsp vegetable oil
4–5 mushrooms, sliced
1 garlic clove, finely chopped
½ red pepper, seeded and
cut into strips
small stalk of broccoli,
broken into florets
7oz fresh udon or yakisoba noodles
(if you cannot find fresh, cook the
dried noodles, drain and rinse in
cold water)
salt, pepper and onion powder
to taste

Takes 15 minutes • Serves 1
(easily doubled)

1 Heat the oil in a medium pot. Add the
mushrooms, garlic, red pepper and broccoli and
stir fry until the vegetables are beginning to soften,
about 4 minutes.
2 Add the noodles. Stir in 1 cup boiling water.
Season with salt, pepper and onion powder
3 Cook the noodles for 2 minutes until they
are tender and piping hot.

• Per serving: 457 calories, protein 16g, carbohydrate 84g, fat
9g, saturated fat 0.2g, fiber 5g, added sugar none, salt 0.02g

Another meal-in-a-bowl soup, full of color and flavor.
You can freeze it for up to one month.

Chunky Fish Chowder

1 large onion, thinly sliced
1lb 2oz potatoes, peeled and
cut into small chunks
1 quart milk
salt & pepper to taste
1 garlic clove, crushed
10oz can corn kernels, drained
1lb skinless smoked fish fillets,
such as haddock
2 tbsp chopped fresh parsley
crusty brown bread, to serve

Takes 30–40 minutes • Serves 4

1 Put the onion and potatoes into a large pot, pour the milk over and season well with freshly ground black pepper. Bring to a boil, cover and simmer for 10 minutes, stirring occasionally.
2 Stir in the garlic, corn and fish, bring back to a boil, cover and simmer for 5 minutes.
3 Flake the fish into bite-size pieces with a fork. Stir in the parsley and season with salt and pepper to taste. Serve with crusty brown bread.

• Per serving: 417 calories, protein 36g, carbohydrate 57g, fat 7g, saturated fat 3g, fiber 3g, added sugar 5g, salt 3.04g

A quick and easy no-cook soup made from supermarket ingredients. It makes an ideal packed lunch.

Cold Tomato Salsa Soup

8 tomatoes (about 1lb 7oz), roughly chopped
½ medium or 1 small red onion, roughly chopped
good handful of fresh cilantro (coriander)
16oz Italian tomato sauce
15oz can cannellini beans, drained
salt & pepper to taste
handful of chopped fresh cilantro and tortilla chips, to serve

Takes 10 minutes • Serves 4

1 Put the tomatoes, onion and cilantro in a food processor and pulse briefly to chop.
2 Put into a large bowl with the tomato sauce and beans, then add ½ cup water. Season with salt and pepper and mix well.
3 Sprinkle with chopped cilantro and serve with tortilla chips.

• Per serving: 141 calories, protein 8g, carbohydrate 26g, fat 1g, saturated fat none, fiber 5g, added sugar 2g, salt 0.84g

Out of season, frozen peas work really well in this soup.
Serve with Italian-style crusty bread.

Chilled Fresh Pea Soup

1oz butter
10oz starchy potatoes,
cut into cubes
a bunch of scallions, thinly sliced
1½ pints vegetable stock
2lb peas in pods, shelled,
or 8oz fresh or frozen peas
6oz plain mild yogurt
a handful of fresh chives, snipped

Takes 30 minutes, plus chilling • Serves 6

1 Melt the butter in a pot, then add the potatoes and stir well. Cover and cook gently for 5 minutes. Stir in the scallions, then add the stock and bring to a boil.
2 Cover and cook for 10 minutes, until the potatoes are just tender. Add the peas and cook for 3 minutes, then puree the soup in a food processor or blender.
3 Pour into a bowl and whisk in the yogurt, then leave to cool. When cool, cover with plastic wrap and chill. Stir in the chives when ready to serve.

• Per serving: 143 calories, protein 7g, carbohydrate 14g, fat 7g, saturated fat 4g, fiber 3g, added sugar none, salt 0.64g

To prepare asparagus, snap off the woody bottom then boil, steam or roast. Parboiling, then roasting, only works for young asparagus.

Roast Asparagus with Garlic

12oz asparagus
2 tbsp olive oil
1 large garlic clove,
cut into very thin slices
1 tbsp large capers in brine,
rinsed and drained
juice of ½ orange
sea salt to taste

Takes 20 minutes •
Serves 4 as a starter

1 Preheat the oven to 400°F. Bring a large pot of water to a boil. Add the asparagus and boil for 2 minutes until crisp but beginning to be tender.
2 Drain and refresh under cold water. Dry on paper towels. Pour the oil into a shallow roasting pan and roll the asparagus in it to coat.
3 Scatter the garlic slivers and capers and roast for 8–10 minutes until the asparagus is just browned and cooked through—test by inserting a knife into a few spears. Sprinkle with orange juice, season with sea salt and serve warm.

• Per serving: 79 calories, protein 3g, carbohydrate 3g, fat 6g, saturated fat 1g, fiber 2g, added sugar none, salt 0.06g

Parma ham fries to a crisp very quickly, and the salty
flavor goes well with most green vegetables.

Beans with Crispy Ham

1lb green beans, trimmed
1 tbsp olive oil
3oz Parma ham or prosciutto,
torn into strips
1 bunch scallions, sliced diagonally
1 tbsp balsamic vinegar
salt & pepper to taste

Takes 20 minutes • Serves 6

1 Bring a pot of water to a boil, add salt and blanch
the beans for 3–4 minutes.
2 Meanwhile, heat the oil in a large frying pan or
wok and cook the ham until crispy. Add the scallions
and vinegar and stir for 1 minute.
3 Drain the beans and add them to the pan. Toss to
coat the beans in oil. Season with salt and pepper
and serve immediately.

• Per serving: 68 calories, protein 6g, carbohydrate 3g, fat 4g,
saturated fat 1g, fiber 2g, added sugar none, salt 0.94g

Butternut squash has a lovely, delicate flavor.
This recipe has a buttery taste without being high in fat.

Baked Butternut Squash

1 butternut squash (about 1lb 8oz)
salt & pepper to taste
½ tsp paprika
3 tbsp snipped fresh chives
3 tbsp mild yogurt or sour cream
1 thick slice of white bread,
crust removed, crumbled
into breadcrumbs
a generous knob of butter, melted
1oz grated parmesan cheese

Takes 1 hour 10 minutes • Serves 2

1 Preheat the oven to 400°F. Halve the squash lengthwise, then scoop out the seeds and fibers and discard. Season the squash well with salt and pepper and put in a roasting pan that is half full of water. Cover with foil and bake for about 40 minutes until tender.

2 Drain, then transfer the squash to a board until cool enough to handle. Scrape the flesh into a bowl, leaving a thin border of flesh on the skin. Mix the paprika, chives and yogurt with the flesh and season with salt and pepper.

3 Pile the mixture into the squash shells. Mix the breadcrumbs with the butter and parmesan and sprinkle on top. Bake for 15 minutes until lightly browned.

• Per serving: 271 calories, protein 13g, carbohydrate 35g, fat 10g, saturated fat 6g, fiber 5g, added sugar none, salt 0.78g

Everyone loves baked potato wedges, and this saucy version is especially popular with children.

Potato Wedges with Tuna

3 large baking potatoes
3 tbsp olive oil
1 leek, sliced
6oz can tuna packed in water, drained
2 X 15oz cans whole stewed tomatoes, with juice, chopped
chili powder to taste
salt & pepper to taste

Takes 35 minutes • Serves 4

1 Preheat the oven to 425°F. Cut the potatoes into wedges and put in a roasting pan. Drizzle on 2 tablespoons of the oil, making sure all the potatoes are covered. Bake for 30 minutes, until crispy on the outside and soft inside.

2 Meanwhile, heat the remaining oil in a pan and saute the leek until softened. Add the tuna, tomatoes and chili powder, breaking the tuna down until well combined with the tomatoes.

3 Cook for a few minutes until hot. Season with salt and pepper and spoon over the potatoes in the roasting pan, mixing gently. Serve immediately.

• Per serving: 264 calories, protein 16g, carbohydrate 32g, fat 9g, saturated fat 1g, fiber 5g, added sugar none, salt 0.76g

Don't let the lengthy cooking time put you off.
The actual work takes only 10 minutes.

Baked Potatoes with Tuna

4 baking potatoes
8oz fat-free cottage cheese with onions and chives
6 oz solid white tuna, packed in water, drained
1 celery stalk, sliced
3 scallions, trimmed and sliced
salt & pepper to taste
Tabasco sauce and green salad, to serve

Takes 1½ hours • Serves 4

1 Preheat the oven to 350°F. Prick the potatoes with a fork. Put them straight on to a rack in the hottest part of the oven for 1–1¼ hours, or until they are soft inside.

2 Meanwhile, mix the cottage cheese with the tuna, celery and scallions. Season with salt and pepper.

3 To serve, cut a deep cross in each baked potato and spoon the filling on top. Sprinkle with a few drops of Tabasco sauce and serve with a green salad.

• Per serving: 237 calories, protein 20g, carbohydrate 39g, fat 1g, saturated fat none, fiber 3g, added sugar none, salt 0.61g

If you can't find smoked trout for this salad,
any firm, white smoked fish will do.

Trout, Beet and Bean Salad

8oz fine green beans, trimmed
4 oz mixed watercress and
arugula
salt & pepper to taste
2 tsp balsamic vinegar
8 oz smoked trout fillets
4 small cooked beets, diced
6 tbsp fat-free farmer's cheese
1–2 tbsp fresh lemon juice
2 tsp bottled creamy
horseradish sauce

Takes 15 minutes • Serves 4

1 Cook the green beans in a pot of lightly salted boiling water for 3–4 minutes until just tender. Drain and refresh in cold water.
2 Put the salad leaves in a large bowl and season with salt and pepper. Pour in the balsamic vinegar and toss well to coat. Arrange the dressed leaves on a serving dish. Flake the trout on to the leaves and top with the cooked beans and diced beets.
3 Mix the farmer's cheese, lemon juice and horseradish sauce and season with salt and pepper. Drizzle over the salad just before serving.

• Per serving: 140 calories, protein 17g, carbohydrate 10g, fat 4g, saturated fat 1g, fiber 3g, added sugar none, salt 1.52g

An easy salad made from ingredients you probably have in the pantry. Perfect when you suddenly want a snack.

Tuna, Bean and Corn Salad

6oz can solid white tuna, drained
6oz can corn, drained
½ red onion, finely chopped
6oz red kidney beans, drained
salt & pepper to taste
2 handfuls mixed salad leaves
1 tbsp olive oil
2 tsp fresh lemon juice
a pinch of mild chili powder
toasted crusty bread, to serve

Takes 10 minutes • Serves 2
(easily doubled)

1 In a large bowl, mix the tuna lightly with the corn, onion and kidney beans. Season well with salt and pepper.
2 Divide the salad leaves between two plates, season with salt and pepper lightly, then pile the tuna salad on top.
3 Drizzle with the olive oil and lemon juice and sprinkle with the chili powder. Serve with toasted crusty bread.

• Per serving: 277 calories, protein 21g, carbohydrate 33g, fat 8g, saturated fat 1g, fiber 6g, added sugar 5g, salt 1.63g

A simple salad of crunchy vegetables in a warm dressing,
served with sticky sushi rice.

Japanese Salad with Rice

8oz sushi rice
1 large white radish (daikon), peeled
2 carrots, peeled
1 small cucumber (about 9oz)
3 tbsp mirin (Japanese sweet
rice wine) or dry sherry
2 tbsp rice wine vinegar
2 tbsp Japanese soy sauce
2 tsp fine sugar
cilantro (coriander) sprigs, to serve

Takes 20 minutes, plus standing • Serves 4

1 Rinse the rice in a sieve under cold water until the water runs clear. Place in a pot and add 1 cup cold water, cover, then bring to a boil. Simmer for 10 minutes without removing the lid. Leave to stand, covered, for 10 minutes.

2 Meanwhile, cut the radish, carrots and cucumber into matchsticks and place in a bowl. Put the remaining ingredients in a small pan and heat gently until steam starts to rise. Pour over the vegetables and marinate for 15 minutes.

3 Divide the rice among four serving plates, spoon the vegetables on top, then drizzle with the dressing. Serve immediately, topped with the cilantro.

• Per serving: 254 calories, protein 5g, carbohydrate 57g, fat 1g, saturated fat 0.03g, fiber 1g, added sugar 3g, salt 1.15g

This is a hearty salad, packed with
interesting textures and flavors.

Warm Potato and Spinach Salad

1lb 9oz new potatoes,
scrubbed and halved
8oz baby spinach leaves
4 thick slices of bacon, trimmed
of excess fat
6oz button mushrooms, thinly sliced
15oz can lima beans, drained
salt & pepper to taste

FOR THE DRESSING
1 garlic clove, crushed
2 tsp wholegrain mustard
2 tsp balsamic vinegar
1 tbsp olive oil

Takes 30 minutes • Serves 4

1 Cook the potatoes in salted boiling water for 8–10
minutes until just tender. Drain and
immediately toss with the spinach leaves, so they
wilt very slightly. Set aside.
2 Broil the bacon for 5–6 minutes until it is very
crisp. Drain on paper towels. Mix all the dressing
ingredients in a large bowl. Add the mushrooms and
lima beans, season with salt and pepper and let
stand for 5 minutes.
3 Add the potatoes, spinach and bacon to the
mushrooms, then toss together. Serve immediately.

• Per serving: 282 calories, protein 14g, carbohydrate 39g, fat
9g, saturated fat 2g, fiber 7g, added sugar none, salt 1.94g

This healthy and colorful alternative to fried eggs is as good
for lunch as it is for breakfast.

Pepper and Egg Sauté

1 tbsp olive oil
1 large onion, finely chopped
2 garlic cloves, crushed
2 yellow peppers, seeded and
finely sliced
10oz green beans, cut
into 2in pieces
8 tbsp white wine
4 ripe tomatoes, diced
4 medium eggs
4 tbsp chopped fresh flatleaf parsley
salt & pepper to taste
crusty bread, to serve

Takes 25 minutes • Serves 4

1 Heat the olive oil in a large pan and saute the
onion and garlic for 2 minutes until softened. Add
the yellow peppers, green beans and white wine.
Cook, stirring, another 2–3 minutes.
2 Add the diced tomatoes and cook for 1–2
minutes until warmed through. Make four hollows in
the vegetable mixture with the back of a spoon.
3 Crack an egg into each one and cook over medium heat for 3–4 minutes until the egg is set to your
liking. Sprinkle with the parsley and season well with
salt and pepper. Serve with crusty bread.

• Per serving: 187 calories, protein 10g, carbohydrate 11g, fat
10g, saturated fat 2g, fiber 4g, added sugar none, salt 0.23g

A no-cook lunch packed with vitamins. Eat immediately,
while the pears and watercress are fresh and crisp.

Ham and Pear Open Sandwiches

3 tbsp thick honey
1 tbsp Dijon mustard
2 tsp dark brown sugar
4 thick slices sourdough rye bread
1 ripe but firm pear
4 slices Parma ham
a large handful of watercress
fresh black pepper

Takes 10 minutes • Serves 2

1 Mix together the honey, mustard and dark brown sugar to a smooth paste.
2 Spread the honey mixture over the bread slices. Cut the pear in half lengthwise without peeling it, and core and discard the seeds. Cut it into thick slices.
3 Cover each piece of bread with slices of pear and top with slices of Parma ham. Add a pile of watercress leaves and grind pepper over the top. Serve immediately.

• Per serving: 315 calories, protein 13g, carbohydrate 58g, fat 5g, saturated fat 1g, fiber 4g, added sugar 23g, salt 2.75g

Spicy falafel, made from chickpeas, make a tasty
filling for a hot pita bread sandwich.

Falafel Pitas

2 × 15oz cans chickpeas, drained
1 small onion, roughly chopped
2 carrots, roughly chopped
1 large garlic clove, roughly chopped
1 tsp ground coriander
1 tsp ground cumin
a small handful of parsley sprigs
salt & pepper to taste
oil, for brushing
6 pita breads
crispy lettuce, cucumber slices and
natural yogurt, to serve

Takes 25 minutes • Serves 6

1 Preheat the broiler. Put the chickpeas into a food processor with the onion, carrots, garlic, coriander, cumin, parsley, salt and pepper. Process briefly to retain some of the chunky texture in the chickpeas. Shape the mixture into six round cakes.
2 Carefully place the falafels on a broiler pan lined with foil. Brush with a little oil. Broil for 4–5 minutes on each side. Meanwhile, toast the pita breads and tear the lettuce into strips.
3 Stuff the hot falafels into the pita breads. Add a small handful of torn lettuce, a few slices of cucumber and a drizzle of natural yogurt. Serve immediately.

• Per serving: 281 calories, protein 12g, carbohydrate 53g, fat 4g, saturated fat 0g, fiber 6g, added sugar none, salt 1.3g

This is a modern version of beans on toast.
Try it topped with stir-fried garlicky greens.

Radicchio, Bean and Chili Crostini

2 tbsp olive oil
1 red onion, thinly sliced
2 garlic cloves, thinly sliced
1 red chili, halved,
seeded and sliced
2 tbsp balsamic vinegar
15oz can cannellini beans,
drained and rinsed
4 tbsp dry white wine
a handful flatleaf parsley,
roughly torn
salt & pepper to taste
4 thick slices crusty Italian bread
2 heads radicchio,
halved lengthwise

Takes 20 minutes • Serves 4

1 Heat 1 tablespoon of the oil in a pan and saute the onion, garlic and chili for 5 minutes, until softened. Stir in the vinegar, beans and wine and cook for 3–4 minutes, until all the liquid has evaporated. Stir in the parsley and season with salt and pepper.
2 Meanwhile, brush the remaining oil over a griddle and heat until starting to smoke. Arrange the bread and radicchio, cut-side down, on top and cook for 1 minute. Remove the radicchio. Turn the bread over and brown the other side.
3 Divide the bread between serving plates and spoon the beans on top. Place the radicchio on top and season with salt and pepper with freshly ground black pepper. Serve immediately.

• Per serving: 302 calories, protein 11g, carbohydrate 38g, fat 12g, saturated fat 1g, fiber 8g, added sugar none, salt 1.15g

Unlike some Thai dishes, these kebabs are not too hot,
just mildly spicy—perfect for a light supper or lunch.

Spicy Thai Fish Kebabs

1 tsp lemon pepper
2 tsp dried flaked coconut
1 tsp vegetable oil
salt & pepper to taste
9oz skinless firm white fish fillets,
cut into long strips
1 yellow pepper, seeded and
cut into chunks
1 onion, cut into chunks
4 cherry tomatoes
cooked jasmine rice, to serve

FOR THE DIP
1 tbsp chopped fresh parsley
½ cup low-fat yogurt
lemon juice, to taste

Takes 20–30 minutes • Serves 2

1 Preheat the oven to 350°F. Line a baking pan with foil and brush lightly with oil.
2 Mix the lemon pepper, coconut and oil in a shallow bowl and season well with salt and pepper. Roll the fish in the spice mixture, then loosely thread it on four skewers. Follow with two to three chunks of pepper and onion per skewer and finish with a cherry tomato.
3 Roast the skewers on the foil for 8–10 minutes, or until the fish is white and opaque. Stir the parsley into the yogurt, then add the lemon juice and season with salt and pepper to taste. Serve with the kebabs and rice.

• Per serving: 215 calories, protein 27g, carbohydrate 18g, fat 5g, saturated fat 1g, fiber 3g, added sugar none, salt 2.07g

Take a few kitchen pantry basics and you can
have supper on the table in about 15 minutes.

Tomato and Olive Spaghetti

12oz spaghetti
1 tbsp olive oil
2 garlic cloves, finely chopped
4 anchovy fillets in oil, drained
15oz can plum tomatoes
4oz pitted black olives,
roughly chopped
3 tbsp capers, rinsed and
roughly chopped
salt & pepper to taste
2 tbsp chopped fresh parsley

Takes 15 minutes • Serves 4

1 Stir the spaghetti into a large pot of salted boiling water and cook for 12–15 minutes, until just tender.
2 Meanwhile, heat the oil in a pan and cook the garlic and anchovies for 2 minutes. Add the tomatoes and cook for 5 minutes, breaking them lightly with a wooden spoon. Stir in the olives and capers and cook 5 minutes more. Season with salt and pepper and stir in the parsley.
3 Drain the pasta well and return to the pot. Stir in the sauce, divide between warmed bowls and serve.

• Per serving: 377 calories, protein 13g, carbohydrate 68g, fat 8g, saturated fat 1g, fiber 4g, added sugar none, salt 1.98g

There's more to spaghetti than tomato sauce.
Try this low-fat sauce made with baby clams.

Seafood Spaghetti

6oz spaghetti
1 tbsp olive oil
2 garlic cloves, finely chopped
15oz can chopped tomatoes
6oz can baby clams, drained
pinch of dried chili flakes
salt & pepper to taste
2 tbsp chopped fresh parsley

Takes 15 minutes • Serves 2
(easily doubled)

1 Cook the spaghetti in a pot of salted boiling water for 10–12 minutes, until tender.
2 Meanwhile, heat the oil in a pan, then saute the garlic for 30 seconds. Add the tomatoes and let them bubble for 2–3 minutes. Add the clams and chili flakes, season with salt and pepper, then stir to heat through.
3 Drain the spaghetti and return to the pot. Stir in the sauce and serve sprinkled with chopped parsley.

• Per serving: 424 calories, protein 21g, carbohydrate 71g, fat 8g, saturated fat 1g, fiber 5g, added sugar none, salt 1.39g

This pasta sauce can be made up to two days in advance and chilled. Or thin it down with stock to make a tasty soup.

Pumpkin and Bean Spaghetti

2 tbsp olive oil
2 onions, thinly sliced
2 garlic cloves, crushed
12oz diced pumpkin or
butternut squash
15oz can chopped tomatoes
14fl oz vegetable stock
12oz spaghetti
15oz can mixed beans in
a mild chili sauce
salt & pepper to taste
a small handful finely grated
parmesan cheese, to serve

Takes 50 minutes • Serves 4

1 Heat the oil in a pot and saute the onions for 8 minutes, until softened. Add the garlic and pumpkin or squash and cook 5 minutes more. Stir in the tomatoes and stock. Bring to a boil, cover and simmer for 15 minutes, until the pumpkin is tender.
2 Meanwhile, cook the spaghetti in a large pot of salted boiling water, according to the package instructions.
3 Add the beans to the pasta sauce and cook for 3–4 minutes. Season with salt and pepper. Drain the spaghetti well, return to the pot, then stir in the sauce. Divide between shallow bowls and serve sprinkled with parmesan cheese.

• Per serving: 477 calories, protein 19g, carbohydrate 88g, fat 8g, saturated fat 1g, fiber 9g, added sugar none, salt 2.01g

If you love garlic, try adding a couple of
chopped cloves to the breadcrumbs.

Spaghetti with Broccoli and Anchovies

12oz spaghetti
12oz broccoli
5 tbsp olive oil
6 anchovies, chopped
2 fresh red chilies, seeded and
finely chopped
4oz white breadcrumbs,
made with stale bread
salt & pepper to taste

Takes 25–30 minutes • Serves 4

1 Cook the spaghetti in a large pot of boiling water,
according to the package instructions. Cut the
broccoli into small florets, thinly slice the thick stalks
and throw into the pot with the pasta for the last 3
minutes of cooking time.
2 Meanwhile, heat 3 tablespoons of olive oil in a
frying pan, add the anchovies and chilies and saute
briefly. Add the breadcrumbs and cook, stirring, for
about 5 minutes, until the crumbs are crunchy and
golden.
3 Drain the spaghetti and return to the pot. Toss
with three-quarters of the crumb mixture, some salt
and pepper and another 2 tablespoons of olive oil.
Serve each portion sprinkled with the remaining
crumbs.

• Per serving: 400 calories, protein 17g, carbohydrate 78g, fat
4g, saturated fat 0.5g, fiber 5g, added sugar none, salt 0.8g

This simple recipe uses just five ingredients and
is excellent for using up tomatoes that are too soft for salad.

Creamy Tomato and Pepper Pasta

2lb ripe tomatoes
1 red pepper
2 garlic cloves
3 tbsp olive oil
salt & pepper to taste
12oz penne or pasta shells
4 tbsp cream
grated parmesan cheese, to serve

Takes 50 minutes • Serves 4

1 Preheat the oven to 400°F. Quarter the tomatoes, roughly chop the pepper (discarding the seeds) and finely chop the garlic. Put them in a roasting pan and drizzle with the olive oil. Season well with salt and pepper.

2 Roast for 30–35 minutes, stirring halfway through, until softened and slightly browned. Meanwhile, cook the pasta in a large pot of salted boiling water for 10–12 minutes, until just tender (follow the package instructions if you are using fresh pasta).

3 Remove the vegetables from the oven and stir in the cream, a spoonful at a time. Bubble up on the stove to reheat, taste and season with salt and pepper if necessary. Stir in the drained pasta and serve with grated parmesan cheese.

• Per serving: 419 calories, protein 13g, carbohydrate 77g, fat 9g, saturated fat 4g, fiber 6g, added sugar none, salt 0.38g

You can rustle up the ingredients for this tasty pasta supper from cans and packages in the kitchen cupboards.

Pasta with Tuna and Tomato

2 tbsp olive oil
1 onion, chopped
2 garlic cloves, finely chopped
15oz can chopped tomatoes
with herbs
½ tsp chili powder
1 tsp sugar
salt & pepper to taste
16oz package bowtie pasta
3.5oz tuna, drained
a handful of basil leaves, optional

Takes 25 minutes • Serves 4

1 Heat the oil in a pan, add the onion and cook for a couple of minutes. Stir in the garlic, tomatoes, chili powder and sugar. Season with salt and pepper and bring to a boil. Stir, then reduce the heat and simmer for 5 minutes.

2 Meanwhile, bring a large pot of salted water to a boil. Add the pasta and cook according to package instructions.

3 Flake the tuna into the sauce and heat through. Drain the pasta, return to the pot and stir in the sauce and basil leaves. Serve with a generous grinding of pepper.

• Per serving: 553 calories, protein 21g, carbohydrate 102g, fat 10g, saturated fat 1g, fiber 5g, added sugar 1g, salt 0.52g

This recipe makes a great vegetarian family supper,
and can easily be halved to serve two.

Summer Veggie Pasta

8oz bowtie pasta
6oz fresh or frozen shelled fava
beans (about 7oz in their pods)
1 tbsp extra-virgin olive oil
1 large onion, finely chopped
2 garlic cloves, chopped
2 large zucchini, cut into sticks
6 ripe plum tomatoes,
cut into wedges
a generous dash of Tabasco
a handful of shredded basil
salt & pepper to taste

Takes 30 minutes • Serves 4

1 Cook the pasta according to the package instructions, adding the fresh fava beans for the last
3 minutes (frozen ones for the last 2 minutes).
2 While the pasta is cooking, heat the oil in a large
pan. Add the onion and cook over medium heat for
1–2 minutes. Stir in the garlic and zucchini, toss
over medium heat for 2–3 minutes, then stir in
the tomatoes and shake in the Tabasco. Stir for 2–3
minutes to soften the tomatoes a little (not too much
or they will get mushy). Drain the pasta and beans.
3 Toss the vegetables and basil into the pasta and
season with salt and pepper. Serve hot, or cold as a
salad with a low-fat dressing).

• Per serving: 284 calories, protein 12g, carbohydrate 51g, fat
5g, saturated fat 1g, fiber 7g, added sugar none, salt 0.1g

Tangy goat's cheese goes wonderfully with the smoky peppers.
Try this dish with spaghetti or pasta shapes too.

Roasted Tomato and Pepper Gnocchi

1lb ripe tomatoes, halved
2 red peppers, cut into strips
2 garlic cloves, unpeeled
2 tbsp olive oil
salt & pepper to taste
16oz fresh gnocchi
4oz goat's cheese
fresh basil leaves and a green salad,
to serve

Takes 25 minutes • Serves 4

1 Preheat oven to 425°F. Put the tomatoes, peppers and garlic and oil in a roasting pan. Sprinkle with salt and stir to coat. Roast for 20 minutes. Just before the tomatoes and peppers are done, cook the gnocchi in salted boiling water for 2–3 minutes, or according to the package instructions.

2 Remove the tomatoes, peppers and garlic from the oven. Squeeze the garlic from its skin and put in a food processor with the tomatoes, peppers and pan juices. Season with salt and pepper. Process for a few seconds for a chunky sauce.

3 Drain the gnocchi and transfer to a bowl. Pour the sauce over the gnocchi and mix gently. Divide between plates, crumble on the cheese and scatter with torn basil leaves. Serve with a green salad.

• Per serving: 326 calories, protein 9g, carbohydrate 50g, fat 11g, saturated fat 1g, fiber 4g, added sugar none, salt 1.6g

Simple ingredients are given a flavor boost with fresh-tasting lemongrass, cilantro and the fiery heat of chopped chili.

Fragrant Rice with Chili Vegetables

8oz jasmine rice
1 stalk lemongrass, finely chopped
salt & pepper to taste
6oz snow peas, halved lengthwise
6oz baby corn, halved lengthwise
2 tomatoes, roughly chopped
1oz fresh cilantro (coriander), finely chopped
1oz dried flaked coconut, lightly toasted
1 red chili, finely chopped
1 tbsp soy sauce
cilantro sprigs, to serve

Takes 45 minutes • Serves 4

1 Half fill the base of a steamer with water. Bring to a boil and cover with the steamer rack and lid. Rinse the rice under cold running water. Drain and put into a heatproof bowl (check that it will fit into the steamer). Add the lemongrass, season with salt and pepper and pour 2 cups of boiling water into the bowl. Put into the steamer and put on the lid. Cook for 30 minutes until the rice has absorbed almost all the water.

2 Arrange the vegetables in the steamer, around the bowl. Cover and steam for 2 minutes.

3 Stir the cilantro, coconut and chili into the rice and divide it between serving plates. Top with the vegetables and drizzle the soy sauce on top. Serve topped with the cilantro sprigs.

• Per serving: 249 calories, protein 7g, carbohydrate 48g, fat 5g, saturated fat 3g, fiber 3g, added sugar none, salt 0.65g

This filling meal, ready in just 25 minutes, uses mostly ingredients you have in the pantry, keeping shopping to a minimum.

Tuna and Tomato Rice

8oz long grain rice
1 tbsp olive oil
2 garlic cloves, finely chopped
1 onion, finely chopped
2 thick sliced bacon, chopped
6oz chestnut mushrooms, sliced
2 × 15oz cans chopped tomatoes
6oz can tuna, drained
salt & pepper to taste
a generous handful of fresh parsley, finely chopped
garlic bread, to serve

Takes 25 minutes • Serves 4

1 Cook the rice in salted boiling water for 10–12 minutes, or as directed on the package.
2 Meanwhile, heat the oil in a pan and saute the garlic, onion and bacon for 5 minutes, stirring often. Add the mushrooms and cook for another 2–3 minutes. Stir in the tomatoes and tuna and season well with salt and pepper. Heat through for 5 minutes.
3 Drain the rice and stir it into the tomato sauce with the parsley, mixing gently. Serve with garlic bread.

• Per serving: 346 calories, protein 19g, carbohydrate 57g, fat 6g, saturated fat 2g, fiber 6g, added sugar 3g, salt 3.52g

Use your microwave to make perfect rice in next to no time. You'll find arborio rice in most supermarkets.

Quick Fish Risotto

1 onion, finely chopped
1 garlic clove, finely chopped
1 vegetable or fish stock cube
9oz arborio rice
9oz smoked white fish fillets, skinned and cut into chunks
1 large cupful of frozen peas
a large knob of butter
salt & pepper to taste
1 lemon, cut into 8 wedges, to serve

Takes 20 minutes • Serves 4

1 Put the onion and garlic in a large microwave-proof bowl with the stock cube and 1 cup boiling water. Stir well, then cover and microwave on High for 3 minutes.
2 Stir in the rice and another 1 cup boiling water, cover and microwave on High for 10 minutes, stirring after 5 minutes.
3 Stir the fish into the rice with the peas and another 1 cup boiling water. Cover and microwave on High for 4 minutes. Check that the rice is cooked if not, cook for another minute. Let stand for 1–2 minutes for the liquid to be absorbed. Stir in the butter and season well with salt and pepper. Serve hot with lemon wedges.

• Per serving: 323 calories, protein 20g, carbohydrate 56g, fat 4g, saturated fat 2g, fiber 3g, added sugar none, salt 3.1g

You'll find flat rice noodles with the oriental foods in the supermarket. Change the vegetables to suit your taste.

Zesty Noodle Stir Fry

5oz flat rice noodles
6 tbsp soy sauce
5 tbsp fresh orange juice
½ tsp finely grated orange zest
1 tsp sugar
½ tsp cornstarch
1 tbsp vegetable or sunflower oil
½ tbsp grated fresh ginger
2 garlic cloves, finely chopped
2 tbsp dry sherry
2 red peppers, seeded and sliced
2 carrots, peeled, cut into fine strips
2 zucchini cut into fine strips
4oz snow peas, sliced
6oz can water chestnuts, sliced
1 bunch scallions, shredded

Takes 40 minutes • Serves 4
(easily halved)

1 Put the noodles in a large bowl, cover with boiling water for 4 minutes, then drain and rinse under cold water.
2 Mix the soy sauce, orange juice and zest, sugar and cornstarch. Heat the oil in a wok, add the ginger and garlic and stir fry for 1 minute. Add the sherry and peppers and stir fry for 1 minute. Add the carrots, zucchini and snow peas and stir fry for 3 minutes. Add the water chestnuts and scallions and stir fry for a minute.
3 Add the soy sauce mixture and noodles and stir fry until hot. Serve immediately.

• Per serving: 240 calories, protein 6g, carbohydrate 47g, fat 3g, saturated fat 0g, fiber 4g, added sugar 1.6g, salt 2.77g

With a package of egg noodles in your kitchen cupboard, you have the basis of a versatile stir fry.

Chicken and Broccoli Noodles

8 oz thin egg noodles
12oz broccoli florets
2 tbsp olive oil
1in piece fresh ginger, grated
4 garlic cloves, finely sliced
2 boneless, skinless chicken breasts, cut into thin strips
1 bunch of scallions, trimmed and cut in half horizontally, large ones cut in half again lengthwise
3 tbsp soy sauce
7fl oz chicken or vegetable stock
black pepper to taste

Takes 20 minutes • Serves 4

1 Cook the noodles in a pot of salted boiling water for 5 minutes, adding the broccoli for the last 2 minutes. Drain.

2 Meanwhile, heat a wok or frying pan until very hot. Add the oil, then stir in the ginger and garlic. Cook for 30 seconds, stirring. Add the chicken strips and cook for 5 minutes, stirring often, until tinged brown. Add the scallions and stir briefly to heat through.

3 Mix the soy sauce and stock together and stir into the pan. Add the drained noodles and broccoli to the pan, season with black pepper and toss everything together. Serve immediately.

• Per serving: 417 calories, protein 30g, carbohydrate 49g, fat 12g, saturated fat 1g, fiber 3g, added sugar none, salt 2.61g

Stretch two chicken breasts to feed four in this unusual salad with a tangy dressing.

Warm Thai Noodle Salad

2 large boneless, skinless chicken breasts
6oz dried medium egg noodles
2 good handfuls of greens, such as Chinese cabbage, finely shredded
2 carrots, cut into thin strips
8 scallions, finely sliced
1 red pepper, seeded and finely sliced
a handful of fresh cilantro (coriander) leaves

FOR THE DRESSING
1 red chili, seeded and finely chopped
2 garlic cloves, finely chopped
1 tbsp finely chopped fresh ginger
2 tbsp soy sauce
juice of 1 lime
2 tbsp olive oil

Takes 30 minutes • Serves 4

1 Preheat the broiler. Put the chicken on a baking sheet and broil for 10–12 minutes without turning, until cooked through. Meanwhile, cook the noodles according to the package instructions. Drain and rinse in cold running water to stop them from sticking together.

2 Mix the vegetables in a bowl. Thinly slice the chicken and add to the bowl, along with the noodles and cilantro leaves.

3 Mix the dressing ingredients together with 2 tablespoons of water, pour over the salad and toss well. Serve immediately.

• Per serving: 336 calories, protein 24g, carbohydrate 40g, fat 10g, saturated fat 1g, fiber 2g, added sugar none, salt 1.7g

SHRIMP, GREEN BEAN AND FETA PASTA SALAD

Shrimp salad of any variety is always popular.

Makes 6 main-course servings.

- 4 ounces green beans, trimmed, each bean cut into 1- to 1½-inch-long pieces
- 8 ounces dried rotini or any similar size pasta
- 1 pound medium cooked shrimp, peeled and deveined
- 2 to 4 tablespoons chopped dill
- 2 tablespoons red-wine vinegar
- 1 tablespoon lemon juice
- 2 tablespoons olive oil
- 4 ounces crumbled feta cheese
- Salt
- Freshly ground black pepper

To blanch green beans: Fill large bowl with ice water. Set aside. In pot of boiling salted water, cook green beans until they turn bright green and start to soften. Immediately transfer beans to ice water to cool completely. Drain beans. Using clean towel, pat beans dry.

To cook pasta: In large pot of salted boiling water, cook pasta until al dente (done but still a little firm to the bite.) Drain in colander. Rinse with cold water until completely cool. Drain until free of excess water. Set aside.

To assemble salad: In large bowl, combine cooked green beans, pasta, shrimp, dill to taste, vinegar, lemon juice, olive oil, feta cheese, salt and pepper to taste. Serve immediately or cover tightly and refrigerate for up to 2 days.

Nutrition information: One serving provides 313 calories, 24 grams protein, 31 grams carbohydrates, 10 grams fat, 164 milligra

THE PIRANHA CLU

LOOK AT THIS NASTY LETTER FROM THE CITY COUNCIL, ENOS!!

EITHER UP M THEY' TO S

ZIPPY THE PINHEA

MR. TOAD?

YES?

©2005 Bill Griffith. World rights reserved. Distributed by King Features Syndicate

JUMBLE

Unscramble these four Jumbles,
re

until al dente.) Drain in colander. Rinse with cold water until completely cool. Drain until free of excess water.

To assemble salad: In large bowl, combine pasta, tuna, chickpeas, onion, parsley, lemon juice and zest, olive oil, salt and pepper to taste. Stir to combine. Serve immediately or cover tightly and refrigerate up to 2 days.

Nutrition information: One serving provides 336 calories, 17 grams protein, 48 grams carbohydrates, 8 grams fat, 5 milligrams cholesterol, 1 gram saturated fat, 370 milligrams sodium, 5 grams dietary fiber.

out a real estate investment or a new item for your home.

LIBRA (Sept. 23-Oct. 22)
★★★★★ How you say something — both the words you use and your tone — can make all the difference in its reception. Your humor and wit cause others to move to your corner. Add allies to your immediate world. **Tonight:** Hang out.

SCORPIO (Oct. 23-Nov. 21)
★★★ Use your financial savvy. Ask questions of someone you respect. You finally get answers through brainstorming and accepting that others have solu-

This tasty rub is also good on pork and lamb.
Try the chicken barbecued too.

Salt and Pepper Fried Chicken

6oz mild plain yogurt
2 tbsp chopped fresh mint
juice of 1 lemon
salt & pepper to taste
a good sprinkling of salt
(sea salt is best)
1 heaped tbsp coarsely crushed
peppercorns (buy them or crush
yourself with a rolling pin)
4 boneless, skinless chicken breasts
2 tbsp oil
new potatoes and salad, to serve

Takes 20 minutes • Serves 4

1 Mix together the yogurt and mint with a squeeze of lemon juice; season with salt and pepper set aside. Mix together the sea salt and peppercorns. Drizzle with a little lemon juice on the chicken breasts, then rub the salt and pepper mixture evenly over each breast.
2 Heat the oil in a large pan. Add the chicken and cook for 6–7 minutes on each side until the chicken is cooked through and golden.
3 Squeeze the remaining lemon juice on the chicken. Serve with the minty yogurt, new potatoes and a salad.

• Per serving: 262 calories, protein 37g, carbohydrate 2g, fat 12g, saturated fat 4g, fiber none, added sugar none, salt 0.56g

This spicy rub makes the skin deliciously crisp. Cajun seasoning is available in most supermarkets.

Cajun-spiced Chicken

2 tbsp all-purpose flour
2 tsp Cajun seasoning
½ tsp salt
4 boneless chicken breasts, about 5oz each
2 tbsp olive oil
tzatziki (yogurt and cucumber salad), mixed salad and new potatoes, to serve

Takes 20 minutes • Serves 4

1 Mix together the flour, Cajun seasoning and salt.
2 Rub both sides of the chicken breasts with 1 tablespoon of the olive oil. Dust each side with the seasoned flour. Heat the remaining oil in a frying pan.
3 Pan fry the coated chicken for 6–7 minutes on each side until cooked and the skin is golden and crispy. Serve with the tzatziki, salad and new potatoes.

• Per serving: 238 calories, protein 35g, carbohydrate 8g, fat 8g, saturated fat 1g, fiber none, added sugar none, salt 0.84g

This sticky glaze turns bland
chicken breasts into something really special.

Glazed Lemon Pepper Chicken

4 skinless, boneless chicken breasts
4 tbsp honey
finely grated zest and juice 1 lemon
2 garlic cloves, crushed
1 tbsp Dijon mustard
2 tsp freshly ground black pepper
1lb 10oz fingerling potatoes
or larger ones, halved
steamed broccoli florets, to serve

Takes 15 minutes, plus marinating • Serves 4

1 Slash each chicken breast two or three times with a sharp knife. In a shallow dish, mix the honey, lemon zest and juice, garlic, mustard and black pepper.

2 Add the chicken and turn to coat. Leave to marinate for 30 minutes or preferably overnight.

3 Preheat the oven to 425°F. Arrange the potatoes and chicken in a single layer in a shallow roasting pan and pour any excess marinade on top. Roast for 25–30 minutes, or until the potatoes are tender and the chicken is cooked. Serve with broccoli and any pan juices.

• Per serving: 339 calories, protein 38g, carbohydrate 44g, fat 3g, saturated fat 1g, fiber 2g, added sugar 11g, salt 0.55g

Removing the skin from chicken breasts reduces
the fat content. Coat them with a tasty glaze instead.

Maple and Orange-glazed Chicken

4 boneless, skinless chicken breasts
3 tbsp maple syrup
1 tbsp wholegrain mustard
grated zest of 1 orange
1 tbsp soy sauce
salad greens with dressing, to serve

Takes 25 minutes • Serves 4
(easily doubled)

1 Make several diagonal slashes across each
chicken breast. Put the other ingredients into a wide,
shallow bowl and mix them together.
2 Add the chicken breasts and turn them in the
mixture until evenly coated. At this point you can
cover the dish with plastic wrap and chill the chicken
for 24 hours, if you don't want to cook the dish
immediately.
3 Preheat the broiler or light the barbecue. Cook the
chicken for 5–6 minutes each side, turning once
and brushing or spooning over more marinade as
you go, until the chicken is browned and glossy.
Serve the chicken on a bed of salad.

• Per serving: 216 calories, protein 26g, carbohydrate 8g, fat
9g, saturated fat 2g, fiber none, added sugar 11g, salt 1g

This simple recipe uses only six ingredients.
It also works well with pork chops.

Chicken with Apples and Cider

2 tbsp oil
4 boneless, skinless chicken breasts
1 onion, cut into wedges
2 eating apples, peeled, cored and
each cut into 8 wedges
1 cup apple cider
½ cup chicken stock
salt & pepper to taste
rice or mashed potatoes, to serve

Takes 35 minutes • Serves 4

1 Heat the oil in a large pan and cook the chicken breasts for 3–4 minutes on each side until golden. Remove from the pan and set aside. Lower the heat slightly and add the onion. Saute, stirring, for 2–3 minutes, until tinged brown. Add the apple and cook over high heat for 5 minutes, until golden.
2 Still over high heat, pour in the cider and let boil for 2 minutes to reduce slightly. Add the stock, stirring to scrape the bits from the bottom of the pan. Lower the heat.
3 Return the chicken to the pan, cover and simmer for 5 minutes, until it is almost cooked. Remove the cover and simmer for 3–4 minutes to thicken the sauce a little. Season with salt and pepper and serve with rice or mashed potatoes.

• Per serving: 269 calories, protein 34g, carbohydrate 12g, fat 7g, saturated fat 1g, fiber 2g, added sugar none, salt 0.36g

A sweet cider blends well with the tangy mustard.
Serve right from the pan for supper.

Cider and Mustard Chicken

2 tbsp vegetable oil
2 onions, sliced
8 skinless, boneless chicken thighs
2 garlic cloves, finely chopped
1 tbsp all-purpose flour
1 cup sweet apple cider
1 tbsp wholegrain mustard
salt & pepper to taste
boiled potatoes and cabbage,
to serve

Takes 40 minutes • Serves 4

1 Heat the oil in a large pan, then saute the onions for 8–10 minutes, stirring often, until browned. Push them to one side of the pan and add the chicken thighs to the pan (with an extra splash of oil, if necessary).
2 Sprinkle with the garlic and cook over high heat for about 10 minutes, turning the chicken thighs until browned all over.
3 Sprinkle the flour over the chicken and cook for 1 minute, stirring. Stir in the cider and boil over medium to high heat for 2 minutes, stirring occasionally to thicken and reduce the sauce slightly. Stir in the mustard, then simmer, covered, for 10 minutes. Season with salt and pepper and serve with potatoes and cabbage.

• Per serving: 260 calories, protein 27g, carbohydrate 12g, fat 10g, saturated fat 2g, fiber 1g, added sugar none, salt 0.5g

This recipe is based on an Indian tikka marinade, but instead of curry powder, it uses red Thai curry paste and chopped cilantro.

Thai-spiced Chicken

8 skinless chicken thighs
12oz natural low-fat yogurt
2–3 tbsp Thai red curry paste
4 tbsp chopped fresh cilantro
(coriander)
salt & pepper to taste
3in piece cucumber
lime wedges and salad greens,
to serve

Takes 55 minutes, plus marinating • Serves 4
(easily doubled)

1 Put the chicken in a shallow dish in one layer. Blend a third of the yogurt, the curry paste and 3 tablespoons of the cilantro. Season well with salt and pour over the chicken, turning the pieces until they are evenly coated. Leave for at least 10 minutes, or in the refrigerator overnight.

2 Preheat the oven to 400°F. Place the chicken pieces on a rack in a roasting pan and roast for 35–40 minutes, until golden. (To cook the chicken on the barbecue, reduce the cooking time to 25–30 minutes.)

3 Blend together the remaining yogurt and cilantro. Finely chop the cucumber and stir into the yogurt mixture. Season with salt and pepper. Serve with the chicken and garnish with wedges of lime and salad greens.

• Per serving: 266 calories, protein 43g, carbohydrate 8g, fat 7g, saturated fat 2g, fiber trace, added sugar none, salt 0.69g

Serve these mildly flavored tasty skewers with jasmine rice
and bok choy stir-fried in a little oil.

Chicken Skewers with Cucumber Dip

1lb 2oz boneless, skinless
chicken breasts
4 tbsp chopped cilantro (coriander)
1 tsp coarsely ground black pepper
juice of 2 limes
1 tsp light brown sugar
2 garlic cloves, crushed
1 tbsp vegetable oil
rice and bok choy, to serve

FOR THE DIP
4fl oz rice vinegar
2 tbsp sugar
1 red chili, seeded and
finely chopped
1 shallot, thinly sliced
1 cucumber

Takes 30 minutes • Serves 4

1 Cut the chicken into thin slices. Mix the cilantro, pepper, lime juice, sugar, garlic and oil. Toss the chicken in this mixture, then thread on to 12 bamboo skewers. (You can make these up to a day ahead and chill until ready to cook.)

2 Make the dip. Heat the vinegar and sugar in a small pan until the sugar has dissolved, then increase the heat and boil for 3 minutes, until slightly syrupy. Remove from the heat and stir in the chili and shallot. Leave to cool.

3 Quarter a 2-inch piece of cucumber, then thinly slice and add to the dip. Cut the rest of the cucumber into thin sticks.

4 Cook the chicken under the broiler for 3–4 minutes on each side, then serve with the dipping sauce, cucumber sticks, rice and bok choy.

• Per serving: 210 calories, protein 31g, carbohydrate 12g, fat 4g, saturated fat 1g, fiber 1g, added sugar 9g, salt 0.22g

There is no need to add flour to thicken the sauce, because as the tomatoes break down, they thicken the juices.

Chicken with Tomatoes and Coriander

1oz butter
4 boneless, skinless chicken breasts, cut into bite-size pieces
1lb fingerling potatoes
2 tsp ground coriander
2 tsp ground cumin
1 cup hot chicken stock
1lb 10oz ripe tomatoes, cut into quarters
salt & pepper to taste
a splash of Tabasco
a squeeze of lemon juice
a handful of chopped fresh cilantro (coriander)

Takes 40 minutes • Serves 4

1 Melt the butter in a large, deep skillet. Add the chicken pieces and potatoes and stir over medium heat for 5–7 minutes until the chicken browns. Add the spices and cook for 1 minute.
2 Pour in the stock and cook, covered, for 10 minutes until the potatoes are just tender. Remove the cover for the last 3 minutes of cooking. Add the tomatoes and cook over medium heat, stirring occasionally, for 5 minutes until the tomatoes are hot and slightly softened.
3 Season with salt and pepper and add a good splash of Tabasco. Squeeze on a little lemon juice and sprinkle with cilantro. Serve hot.

• Per serving: 325 calories, protein 38g, carbohydrate 26g, fat 8g, saturated fat 4g, fiber 3g, added sugar none, salt 0.71g

This colorful sweet and sour stir fry is
great with rice or noodles.

Chinese Chicken with Pineapple

1 tbsp vegetable oil
1 garlic clove, finely chopped
4 boneless, skinless chicken
breasts, cut into bite-size pieces
8oz can pineapple chunks
in natural juice
2 carrots, cut into thin sticks
1 tbsp cornstarch
juice of 1 lemon
2 tbsp tomato paste
3 tbsp light soy sauce
bunch of scallions, trimmed
and halved lengthwise
rice or noodles, to serve

Takes 25 minutes • Serves 4

1 Heat the oil in a wok or frying pan. Add the garlic,
stir briefly, then add the chicken. Cook, stirring, for
10 minutes.
2 Drain the pineapple chunks (save the juice). Add
them to the pan, along with the carrots. Cook,
stirring, for 2–3 minutes.
3 Add enough water to the reserved pineapple juice
to make 7fl oz. Mix the cornstarch with the lemon
juice, then stir in the tomato paste, soy sauce and
diluted pineapple juice. Pour over the chicken and
add the scallions. Cook for 2 minutes more, stirring.
Serve immediately with rice or noodles.

• Per serving: 525 calories, protein 42g, carbohydrate 82g, fat
5g, saturated fat 1g, fiber 2g, added sugar none, salt 1.99g

Adding a good splash of soy sauce as the chicken cooks
helps it brown evenly and boosts the flavor.

Chicken and Broccoli Stir Fry

1oz butter
1lb boneless, skinless chicken
breasts, cut into thin strips
3 tbsp dark soy sauce
12oz broccoli, broken into
small florets
8oz green beans, halved
1 bunch scallions,
cut into long slices
2 tsp cornstarch
juice of 2 oranges
1oz fresh basil, roughly torn
rice or noodles, to serve

Takes 30 minutes • Serves 4
(easily halved)

1 Heat the butter in a wok or large frying pan. Add the chicken strips and a splash of soy sauce and cook for 5 minutes, stirring, until the chicken starts to brown.
2 Stir in the broccoli, green beans and half the scallions and cook for 3 minutes, until just cooked.
3 Mix the cornstarch with the orange juice and remaining soy sauce. Pour into the pan and cook for about 1 minute, stirring, until just thickened. Scatter in the basil and remaining scallions. Serve with rice or noodles.

• Per serving: 273 calories, protein 40g, carbohydrate 11g, fat 8g, saturated fat 4g, fiber 4g, added sugar none, salt 2.4g

There's very little shopping required
for this simple dish.

Spicy Chicken and Apricot Stew

2 tbsp oil
8 boneless, skinless chicken thighs,
cut into chunks
1 large onion, sliced
2 tsp all-purpose flour
2 tsp ground cumin
2 tsp ground coriander
1 tsp paprika
2 cups chicken stock
12 dried apricots
salt & pepper to taste
rice and peas, to serve

Takes 1 hour • Serves 4

1 Heat half the oil in a large pan, add the chicken
and cook for 7 minutes until golden. Remove and set
aside. Add the remaining oil and the onion and cook
for 5 minutes until browned. Return the chicken to
the pan.
2 Sprinkle in the flour and spices and cook, stirring,
for 1–2 minutes. Slowly pour in the stock, stirring,
so it sizzles and the sauce turns a rich color. Simmer
for 15 minutes.
3 Stir in the apricots and simmer for a 15 minutes
more. Taste and season with salt and pepper. Serve
with rice and peas.

• Per serving: 349 calories, protein 41g, carbohydrate 20g, fat
12g, saturated fat 3g, fiber 3g, added sugar none, salt 1.59g

Big, juicy prunes and a variety of spices
make this dish flavorful and exciting.

Spiced Prune Chicken

2 tsp olive oil
1 onion, chopped
1 garlic clove, finely chopped
1 tsp turmeric
½ tsp ground cinnamon
½ tsp ground coriander
½ tsp ground ginger
3 boneless, skinless chicken
breasts, sliced into strips
10oz can chicken stock
2 tbsp tomato paste
salt & pepper to taste
6oz pitted prunes, halved
9oz couscous
handful of chopped fresh cilantro
(coriander), to serve

Takes 45 minutes • Serves 4

1 Heat the oil in a deep skillet. Add the onion and cook for 5 minutes, until just golden. Add the garlic and cook for a minute only, then add the spices and stir for a minute. Add the chicken strips and cook for 4–5 minutes until browned.

2 Add the stock and tomato paste, and season with salt and pepper. Cook for 15–20 minutes, adding the prunes for the last 5 minutes.

3 Meanwhile, cook the couscous according to the package instructions; keep warm. Divide the chicken and prunes between plates, sprinkle with cilantro and serve with the couscous.

• Per serving: 360 calories, protein 32g, carbohydrate 52g, fat 4g, saturated fat 1g, fiber 3g, added sugar 15g, salt 0.5g

Turkey is one of the cheapest meats you can buy and is really low in fat, with just 1.75g fat per 100g of skinless cooked meat.

Cajun Turkey Steaks

1lb small new potatoes
8oz green beans, trimmed and thickly sliced
2 tbsp Cajun seasoning
4 turkey breast fillets
3 tbsp olive oil
finely grated zest and juice 1 lemon
1 garlic clove, crushed
3 firm tomatoes, seeded and cut into chunks

Takes 30 minutes • Serves 4

1 Boil the potatoes for 8 minutes. Add the green beans, cover and cook 4 minutes more.
2 Meanwhile, sprinkle the Cajun seasoning on both sides of each turkey fillet. Heat 1 tablespoon of oil in a large, shallow skillet and pan fry the turkey for 3–4 minutes on each side, until they start to blacken. Add the lemon zest and juice, and boil briefly to reduce slightly.
3 Drain the potatoes and beans. Warm the remaining oil in the pan; stir in the vegetables, garlic and tomatoes. Cook for 1–2 minutes, tossing until the vegetables are just coated. Serve with the turkey and pan juices.

• Per serving: 326 calories, protein 34g, carbohydrate 23g, fat 12g, saturated fat 2g, fiber 3g, added sugar none, salt 0.21g

This hot turkey salad is easily doubled for a crowd.
Try it in sandwiches, too.

Barbecue Turkey Strips

2 tbsp dark brown sugar
4 tbsp honey
4 tbsp soy sauce
1lb boneless turkey strips
2 tbsp olive oil
2 tbsp lemon juice
2 tsp fine sugar
salt & pepper to taste
1 romaine lettuce, torn into pieces
2 large carrots, cut into sticks
4oz fresh beansprouts

Takes 35 minutes, plus marinating • Serves 4

1 Mix the brown sugar, half the honey and half the soy sauce in a shallow dish. Add the turkey strips and stir to coat. Cover and leave to marinate for 30 minutes.

2 Thread the turkey strips on to eight skewers (soak wooden ones for 20 minutes before using to prevent them from burning) and cook under the broiler or barbecue for 6 minutes on each side.

3 Whisk the remaining honey and soy sauce with the olive oil, lemon juice and sugar. Season with salt and pepper and toss with the lettuce and vegetables. Pile onto four plates and put the turkey on top. Serve immediately.

• Per serving: 318 calories, protein 29g, carbohydrate 37g, fat 7g, saturated fat 1g, fiber 2g, added sugar 29g, salt 2.91g

Keep the heat high while cooking the turkey so it sizzles to a good brown color. This dramatically enhances the flavor.

Sweet and Sour Turkey

1 tbsp vegetable oil
10oz turkey strips, cut into smaller strips if necessary
12 oz mixed baby carrots, corn and snow peas
1 red pepper, seeded and sliced
8oz beansprouts
finely grated zest and juice of 1 small orange
3 tbsp soy sauce
1 tsp honey
2 tsp cornstarch
2 garlic cloves, finely chopped
cooked rice or noodles, to serve

Takes 20–25 minutes • Serves 4

1 Heat the oil in a wok or frying pan and pan fry the turkey for 3 minutes, stirring, until browned.
2 Add the baby vegetables and pepper and cook for 4 minutes. Stir in the beansprouts.
3 Mix the orange zest and juice, soy sauce, honey, cornstarch and garlic together. Pour over the stir fry and let it bubble, stirring. When the sauce has thickened, serve with rice or noodles.

• Per serving: 411 calories, protein 24g, carbohydrate 68g, fat 7g, saturated fat 1g, fiber 4g, added sugar 3g, salt 1.87g

Ground turkey is ideal for low-fat burgers.
Don't overcook them or they will be dry.

Spicy Turkey Burgers

1lb ground turkey
1 tbsp dark soy sauce
1–2 tbsp sweet chili sauce
zest and juice of 1 lemon
2 scallions, finely chopped
salt & pepper to taste
tzatziki (yogurt and cucumber
salad), green salad and new
potatoes, to serve

Takes 35 minutes • Serves 4

1 Mix the ground turkey, dark soy sauce, sweet chili sauce, lemon zest and juice, scallions and plenty of salt and freshly ground black pepper until they are well combined.

2 Divide the mixture into four equal portions and shape into burgers.

3 Cook in a preheated broiler for 8 minutes on each side until cooked through. If you want to barbecue them, cook away from the direct heat of the coals for 6–8 minutes, turning frequently until just beginning to char. Serve with the tzatziki, mixed green salad and new potatoes.

• Per serving: 125 calories; protein 26g, carbohydrate 1g, fat 2g, saturated fat 1g, fiber none, added sugar 1g, salt 1.13g

Substitute ground turkey for ground beef
to make a low-fat pasta sauce.

Turkey Bolognese

2 tbsp vegetable oil
1 large onion, chopped
2 garlic cloves, finely chopped
1lb 2oz ground turkey
15oz can chopped tomatoes
2 tbsp tomato paste
1 cup chicken or beef stock
12oz spaghetti
1 large zucchini, finely chopped
6 tomatoes, seeded and chopped
salt & pepper to taste
a small handful of chopped parsley,
to serve

Takes 40 minutes • Serves 4

1 Heat the oil in a large saucepan and saute the onion and garlic for 4–5 minutes over low heat until softened. Stir in the turkey and cook for 5 minutes, stirring frequently. Stir in the chopped tomatoes, tomato paste and stock. Bring to a boil, then simmer, uncovered, for 10 minutes.

2 Meanwhile, cook the spaghetti according to the package instructions. Stir the zucchini and fresh tomatoes into the sauce and simmer for 5–6 minutes. Season with salt and pepper.

3 Drain the pasta and divide among four plates. Spoon the sauce on top and serve, scattered with parsley.

• Per serving: 546 calories, protein 43g, carbohydrate 76g, fat 10g, saturated fat 2g, fiber 6g, added sugar none, salt 0.75g

Skirt steak is mainly used for braising, but cooked this way you'll get succulent meat at a low price.

Barbecued Balsamic Beef

1lb 5oz thick piece
beef skirt or rump steak
2 shallots, very finely chopped
2 tbsp balsamic vinegar,
plus a little extra
salt & pepper to taste
1lb 2oz new potatoes
8 oz washed spinach
2 tbsp olive oil, plus a little extra

Takes 30 minutes, plus marinating • Serves 4

1 Put the beef in a wide, shallow dish and rub it all over with the shallots and balsamic vinegar. Season with salt and pepper and leave to marinate for 20 minutes.

2 Slice the potatoes and cook in salted boiling water for 12–15 minutes, until just tender. Add the spinach and cover the pan for a couple of minutes to wilt the spinach. Drain well, toss in 2 tablespoons of olive oil, and season with salt and pepper. Keep warm.

3 Meanwhile, broil or barbecue the beef for 6–8 minutes on each side for skirt steak or 3–4 minutes each side for rump steak, depending on the thickness. Remove and cover with foil for 5 minutes. Uncover and slice thinly across the grain. Serve piled on top of the potatoes and spinach, sprinkled with a little extra vinegar and olive oil.

• Per serving: 324 calories, protein 37g, carbohydrate 23g, fat 10g, saturated fat 3g, fiber 2.6g, added sugar none, salt 0.49g

This recipe works really well with
lean pork cutlets, too.

Steak with Mustard and Vegetables

1lb new potatoes,
halved lengthwise
12oz broccoli florets
finely grated zest and
juice of 2 oranges
2 garlic cloves, crushed
1 tbsp wholegrain mustard
2 tbsp honey
2 small orange or yellow peppers,
cored, seeded and
cut into chunks
1 tsp vegetable oil
4 lean, thin frying steaks
salt & pepper to taste

Takes 25 minutes • Serves 4

1 Cook the potatoes in lightly salted boiling water for 5–6 minutes. Add the broccoli, return to a boil, and cook for 2–3 minutes or until tender. Drain well, set aside and keep warm.

2 Add the orange zest and juice to the pan, with the garlic, mustard and honey. Bring to a boil. Add the peppers. Cook on high heat until the juices start to thicken, about 1–2 minutes. Add the vegetables and keep warm.

3 Heat a griddle pan. Brush the steaks with the oil and season with salt and pepper on both sides. Put in the pan and press with a spatula. Cook for 2 minutes, turn over and cook 1–2 minutes more. Serve with the vegetables and their pan juices.

• Per serving: 317 calories, protein 34g, carbohydrate 31g, fat 7g, saturated fat 2g, fiber 5g, added sugar 6g, salt 0.4g

This rich, fruity casserole is perfect served with fluffy celeriac and mashed potato.

Beef with Apricots

14oz extra lean stewing beef, cut into cubes
salt & pepper to taste
2 large onions, chopped
4 garlic cloves, crushed
4oz dried apricots, halved
2oz sundried tomato halves (not packed in oil), roughly chopped
15oz can chopped tomatoes

FOR THE POTATOES
1lb starchy potatoes, peeled and cut into small chunks
1 small celeriac, about 1lb 7oz, peeled and cut into small chunks
3½fl oz skim milk
a pinch of nutmeg
salt & pepper to taste

Takes 1½ hours • Serves 4

1 In a non-stick pan, dry-fry the beef in two batches on high heat until browned. Season with salt and pepper, then set aside.

2 Saute the onions and garlic on low heat for 4 minutes (add water if they stick). Return the beef to the pan. Add the apricots, sundried tomatoes, tomatoes and 2 cups water, bring to a boil, and simmer for 1 hour, stirring occasionally.

3 About 25 minutes before the end of cooking, boil the potatoes and celeriac. Drain, add the milk, and mash until smooth. Add the nutmeg, season with salt and pepper and serve with the beef.

• Per serving: 360 calories, protein 31g, carbohydrate 47g, fat 7g, saturated fat 2g, fiber 12g, added sugar none, salt 0.98g

An easy one-pot meal.

Be sure to choose lean lamb, trimmed of fat.

Springtime Lamb Stew

1 tbsp olive oil
12 shallots, peeled
12oz trimmed diced lamb
12oz new potatoes, scrubbed
and cut into chunks
12 baby carrots, trimmed and peeled
½ cup white wine
9fl oz vegetable stock
3 bay leaves
6oz can chopped tomatoes
salt & pepper to taste
4oz frozen peas
1 tbsp fresh chopped parsley
crusty bread, to serve

Takes 1 hour 10 minutes • Serves 4

1 Heat the oil in a large saucepan and add the shallots and lamb. Saute over medium heat until they are starting to brown, about 8–10 minutes.

2 Add the potatoes, carrots, white wine, stock, bay leaves and tomatoes to the pan. Season with salt and pepper and bring to a boil. Cover the pan and leave the stew to simmer gently over medium heat for 25–30 minutes, until the vegetables and lamb are tender.

3 Stir in the peas and cook for another 2–3 minutes, until cooked. Scatter in the parsley, adjust the seasoning and serve with crusty bread.

• Per serving: 291 calories, protein 23g, carbohydrate 21g, fat 11g, saturated fat 4g, fiber 6g, added sugar none, salt 0.58g

A mildly spicy chili with red lentils
replacing the more usual kidney beans.

Lamb and Lentil Chili

1 large onion, finely chopped
2 garlic cloves, crushed
6 oz can chopped tomatoes
1 small eggplant, about 10oz,
cut into ½in cubes
5oz red split lentils
10oz lean diced lamb
1 tsp turmeric
2 tsp mild chili powder
2 tsp ground cumin
1 tsp ground coriander
1 tsp light brown sugar
1 tbsp lemon juice
salt & pepper to taste
small bunch fresh cilantro
(coriander) or
mint, roughly chopped
9fl oz low-fat plain yogurt
basmati rice, to serve

Takes 1¼ hours • Serves 4

1 Put the onion and garlic into a large saucepan with 3½fl oz water. Bring to a boil and cook for 5 minutes, until soft and nearly all the water has been absorbed.

2 Add the tomatoes, eggplant, lentils, lamb, turmeric, chili powder, cumin, coriander, sugar, lemon juice and 2 cups water. Bring to a boil, cover and simmer for 1 hour, until tender.

3 Season well with salt and pepper and stir in most of the cilantro or mint and half the yogurt. Immediately remove from the heat. Serve with basmati rice and the remaining yogurt spooned on top. Sprinkle with the remaining cilantro or mint.

• Per serving: 305 calories, protein 28g, carbohydrate 32g, fat 8g, saturated fat 4g, fiber 4g, added sugar none, salt 0.4g

This is a very adaptable recipe, impressive enough to cook if you have friends visiting and are short of time.

Pork with Pine Nuts

1lb 2oz boneless pork loin
seasoned flour, for coating
a good handful flatleaf parsley
2tbsp olive oil
1oz pine nuts
grated zest of ½ lemon and
juice of a whole lemon
1 tbsp honey
pappardelle or tagliatelle and salad,
to serve

Takes 25 minutes • Serves 4

1 Cut the pork into ¾-inch thick slices. Toss in seasoned flour to coat very lightly, and shake off excess. Coarsely chop the parsley. Heat 1 tablespoon of olive oil in a large skillet pan, add the pork in a single layer and pan fry for 3 minutes on each side, or until browned. Remove and keep warm.

2 Add another tablespoon of oil to the pan, add the pine nuts and cook until lightly browned, then stir in the lemon zest, juice and honey. Boil briefly, stirring to make a sauce.

3 Return the pork to the pan and scatter the parsley. Cook for 3 minutes, turning the pork, until thoroughly reheated. Serve with pappardelle or tagliatelle and salad.

• Per serving: 212 calories, protein 28g, carbohydrate 4g, fat 9g, saturated fat 2g, fiber none, added sugar 4g, salt 0.2g

Pork loin is low in fat and cooks quickly.
Here it's used in a mild curry.

Spicy Pork and Eggplant

1½ tbsp olive oil
2 onions, sliced
1 small eggplant (about 9oz), trimmed and diced
1lb 2oz boneless pork loin, trimmed of any fat and sliced
2 sweet red peppers, seeded and cut into chunky strips
2–3 tbsp mild curry powder
15oz can plum tomatoes
salt & pepper to taste
cooked basmati rice, to serve

Takes 35 minutes • Serves 4

1 Heat the oil in a large non-stick frying pan with a cover. Add the onions and eggplant and saute for 8 minutes, stirring frequently, until soft and golden brown.

2 Add the pork and cook for 5 minutes, stirring occasionally, until it starts to brown. Mix in the pepper strips and stir fry for about 3 minutes, until soft.

3 Sprinkle in the curry powder. Stir fry for a minute, then pour in the tomatoes and ½ cup water. Stir vigorously, cover the pan and leave to simmer for 5 minutes until the tomatoes break down to form a thick sauce (you can add a drop more water if the mixture gets too thick). Season with salt and pepper and serve with basmati rice.

• Per serving: 293 calories, protein 31g, carbohydrate 16g, fat 11g, saturated fat 2g, fiber 6g, added sugar none, salt 0.4g

In this easy recipe, everything is
cooked together in one pan.

Pork with Roasted Vegetables

4 medium parsnips,
quartered lengthwise
1 butternut squash (about 1lb 7oz)
peeled, seeded and cut into
chunks
2 red onions, each cut
into 8 wedges
1 tbsp olive oil
salt & pepper to taste
grated zest of 1 lemon
2 tsp dried mixed Italian herbs
1lb 2oz lean pork tenderloin,
in one or two pieces
1 medium cooking apple
14fl oz chicken stock

Takes 1½ hours • Serves 4

1 Preheat the oven to 400°F. Put the vegetables in a roasting pan. Drizzle with the olive oil. Season with salt and pepper and toss together.
2 On a plate, mix the lemon zest and Italian herbs. Roll the pork in the mix and place on top of the vegetables. Roast for 40–50 minutes.
3 Peel and core the apple. Cut into chunks. Put in the roasting pan. Add the stock and cook 15–20 minutes more. Cut the pork into thick slices and serve with the vegetables and pan juices spooned on top.

• Per serving: 397 calories, protein 34g, carbohydrate 45g, fat 10g, saturated fat 2g, fiber 12g, added sugar none, salt 0.85g

A colorful combination of pork and fruit with a sweet and tangy glaze is a perfect accompaniment to the mellow red cabbage.

Pork Skewers with Red Cabbage

FOR THE CABBAGE
1lb red cabbage, shredded
½ cup ginger beer, wine or stock
2 tbsp soft dark brown sugar
2 tbsp white wine vinegar
2in fresh ginger root, finely chopped

FOR THE PORK
14oz lean pork tenderloin, cut into 24 pieces
2 sweet apples, cut into 8 wedges
salt & pepper to taste
2 tbsp honey
2 tbsp wholegrain mustard
6 tbsp half-and-half
sliced boiled potatoes, to serve

Takes 1 hour 20 minutes • Serves 4

1 Put the cabbage in a large pan with the other cabbage ingredients. Toss over high heat for 5 minutes. Simmer, covered, over low heat for 1 hour, stirring occasionally.

2 Meanwhile, alternate three pieces of pork and two apple wedges on each of eight skewers. Season with salt and pepper. Gently heat the honey and mustard in a small pan. About 15 minutes before the cabbage is cooked, heat the broiler. Cover the broiler pan with foil. Arrange the skewers on top. Brush with the mustard mix and broil for 5–6 minutes. Turn, brush again and broil for 5–6 minutes until cooked.

3 Add the cream to the mustard glaze and heat gently. Arrange the cabbage on plates, put the skewers on top and spoon the pan juices on top. Drizzle with the glaze and serve with sliced potatoes.

• Per serving: 352 calories, protein 25g, carbohydrate 33g, fat 10g, saturated fat 10g, fiber 4g, added sugar 16g, salt 0.59g

Here's a low-fat version of an old favorite.
Be sure to choose the best sausages you can find.

Toad in the Hole

1 red onion, cut into wedges,
layers separated
8 thick low-fat pork sausages
1 tsp olive oil

FOR THE BATTER
4oz all-purpose flour
1 medium egg
1 cup skim milk
2 tsp wholegrain mustard
1 tsp fresh thyme leaves
salt & pepper to taste
steamed carrots and cabbage,
to serve

Takes 1 hour 20 minutes • Serves 4

1 Preheat the oven to 400°F. Put the onions in a small shallow non-stick pan (about 9 × 12 inch). Arrange the sausages on top of the onions, then add the oil and roast for 20 minutes.
2 While they are roasting, make the batter. Sift the flour into a bowl, crack the egg into the center and beat in the milk a little at a time until it makes a smooth batter. Stir in the mustard and thyme and season with salt and pepper.
3 Pour the batter quickly into the pan and return to the oven for 40 minutes, until the batter is risen and golden. Serve with steamed carrots and cabbage.

• Per serving: 293 calories, protein 23g, carbohydrate 36g, fat 7g, saturated fat 2g, fiber 1g, added sugar none, salt 2.36g

This zingy way with ham is surprisingly healthy. Lean steaks are
served with nutritious bulghar wheat and green vegetables.

Sticky Glazed Ham Steaks

3oz bulghar wheat
3oz fresh or frozen peas
(8oz in the pod)
1 large leek, thinly sliced
1 orange, halved
1 tbsp Worcestershire sauce
1 tbsp honey
1 tsp Dijon mustard
salt & pepper to taste
2 lean ham steaks
1 tbsp mint sauce

Takes 30 minutes • Serves 2

1 Preheat the broiler. Put the bulghar and 16fl oz
cold water into a large saucepan, bring to a boil and
simmer for 8 minutes. Toss in the peas and leek and
boil gently for 3–5 minutes more, until soft.
2 While the bulghar cooks, make the glaze. Squeeze
the juice of one half orange into a pan, stir in the
Worcestershire sauce, honey and mustard and
simmer for 2 minutes until sticky. Season the steaks
with pepper only, put them on the broiler pan and
broil for 5–6 minutes on each side, brushing
frequently with the glaze.
3 When the bulghar is cooked, drain, season well
with salt and pepper and fork in the mint sauce.
Cut each steak in half and serve on the bulghar, with
the remaining orange half cut into segments.

• Per serving: 465 calories, protein 45g, carbohydrate 55g, fat
8g, saturated fat 2g, fiber 5g, added sugar 7g, salt 6.89g

A simple dish packed with healthy vegetables.
You could use leftover ham, but make sure it's lean.

Ham and Vegetable Casserole

2 tbsp olive oil
1 large onion, chopped
1lb 2oz waxy new potatoes, halved
1 red pepper, seeded and
cut into chunks
1lb 2oz ripe tomatoes, quartered
½ cup vegetable or chicken stock
1 tsp dried or 1 tbsp chopped
fresh thyme
salt & pepper to taste
3 zucchini, about 13oz total
weight, thickly sliced
6oz thick sliced ham,
cut into strips
a handful of chopped fresh parsley

Takes 45 minutes • Serves 4

1 Heat the oil in a large saucepan. Add the onion and cook, stirring often, for 8 minutes or until golden. Add the potatoes, pepper, tomatoes, stock and thyme. Season well with salt and pepper.
2 Cover and cook for 25 minutes, stirring from time to time until the potatoes are almost tender and the tomatoes have begun to break down to form a sauce.
3 Add the zucchini and simmer for 5 minutes. Stir in the ham and parsley and heat through. Season with salt and pepper and serve.

• Per serving: 272 calories, protein 16g, carbohydrate 34g, fat 9g, saturated fat 2g, fiber 5g, added sugar none, salt 1.35g

If you don't have camembert, use crumbled stilton,
grated gruyère or even aged cheddar cheese instead.

Ham, Leek and Camembert

2 cups chicken or vegetable stock
1lb 9oz scrubbed, unpeeled
potatoes, thickly sliced
1lb leeks (about 2 medium), sliced
4oz thin-sliced ham
salt & pepper to taste
4 oz camembert cheese,
thinly sliced

Takes 25 minutes • Serves 4

1 In a large pot, heat the stock to boiling, then add
the potatoes. Cook for 15 minutes until just tender,
adding the leeks for the last 5 minutes of cooking
time. Drain, reserving 4 tablespoons of the stock.
2 Preheat the broiler. Layer the sliced potatoes and
leeks with the ham in a shallow heatproof dish and
season with salt and pepper between the layers.
3 Pour on the reserved stock. Lay the cheese on
top, then broil for 5 minutes until the cheese has
melted and is beginning to brown. Serve
immediately.

• Per serving: 280 calories, protein 17g, carbohydrate 34g, fat
9g, saturated fat 5g, fiber 5g, added sugar none, salt 1.81g

Choose thin fish fillets so they cook
quickly, before the pesto burns.

Herbed Cod Grills

4 tbsp natural low-fat yogurt
2 tbsp sundried tomato pesto
2 tbsp chopped fresh parsley or dill
2 cod or haddock fillets, about
6oz each, skinned
salad and crusty bread, to serve

Takes 15 minutes • Serves 2
(easily doubled)

1 Preheat the broiler. Mix the yogurt, pesto
and 1 tablespoon of the parsley or dill. Season with
salt and pepper and pour over the fish fillets in a
shallow ovenproof or microwaveable dish, covering
them completely.
2 Broil for 4–5 minutes without turning ,
until the fish fillets are cooked through to the middle.
Or cover the dish with plastic wrap and microwave
on High for 3 minutes.
3 Sprinkle the remaining parsley or dill over the dish
and serve with salad and crusty bread.

• Per serving: 247 calories, protein 36g, carbohydrate 3g, fat
10g, saturated fat 4g, fiber 3g, added sugar none, salt 0.53g

Cod cooks very quickly, so time it carefully—
just a few minutes too much can make it tough and dry.

Spiced Cod with Crispy Onions

4 cod fillets, 5oz each
6 oz mild plain yogurt
1 tbsp tikka masala or curry paste
2 tbsp chopped fresh ginger
juice of ½ lemon
salt & pepper to taste
8oz long-grain rice
5oz green beans, halved
1 tbsp vegetable oil
1 small onion, finely sliced

Takes 25 minutes, plus marinating • Serves 4

1 Put the fish in a single layer in a shallow heatproof dish. Mix together the yogurt, curry paste, half the ginger, and lemon juice. Season with salt and pepper. Pour over the fish, turning to coat. Set aside for 30 minutes.

2 Preheat the broiler. Cook the rice in boiling water for 12–15 minutes, adding the green beans for the last 4 minutes. Broil the fish in its marinade for 8–10 minutes, until the cod is cooked.

3 Meanwhile, heat the oil in a pan. Saute the onion and remaining ginger for 8 minutes over medium heat until golden and crisp. Drain on paper towels. Drain the rice well. Serve the fish with the marinade, rice and green beans. Top with the fried onions and ginger.

• Per serving: 408 calories, protein 34g, carbohydrate 49g, fat 10g, saturated fat 3g, fiber 1g, added sugar none, salt 0.46g

Pan-fried fish needs a light dusting of flour to protect it from the fierce heat, and it makes a tasty, golden crust.

Cod with Lemon and Parsley

2 cod fillets, about 6oz each
seasoned flour
1 lemon
1oz butter
salt & pepper to taste
1 heaped tbsp chopped parsley
new potatoes and salad greens or green beans, to serve

Takes 20 minutes • Serves 2

1 Coat the cod fillets with the flour, dusting off any excess. Squeeze the juice from the lemon.
2 Heat half the butter in a pan. When it is bubbling, add the fish and cook over a fairly high heat until the underside is done, about 4–5 minutes. Using a wide spatula, turn the fillets carefully and brown the other side. When the fish is just cooked (the flesh will start to flake and become opaque), add the remaining butter to the pan. When it is bubbling, stir in the lemon juice and season with salt and pepper.
3 Let the sauce bubble until it is slightly thickened, then stir in the parsley. Serve with new potatoes and salad or green beans.

• Per serving: 277 calories, protein 34g, carbohydrate 9g, fat 12g, saturated fat 7g, fiber 1g, added sugar none, salt 0.77g

Mixed pepper antipasto salad is available in jars in
most supermarkets and delicatessens.

Mediterranean Cod

1lb 10oz starchy potatoes
2 tbsp olive oil
salt & pepper to taste
4 cod fillets, 5oz each
8oz mushrooms
8 tbsp mixed pepper antipasto salad
2 tbsp freshly grated
parmesan cheese

Takes 1 hour • Serves 4

1 Preheat the oven to 400°F. Cut the potatoes into
wedges and put in a roasting pan. Drizzle with the
olive oil and stir well. Season with salt and pepper.
Cook in the middle of the oven for 45–50 minutes,
stirring halfway through, until the potatoes are
golden, crisp and cooked through.
2 Meanwhile, put the cod fillets in an ovenproof dish
in a single layer. Season well with salt and
pepper well. Slice the mushrooms and scatter
over the fish.
3 Spread the mixed pepper antipasto on top of the
mushrooms. Put the fish in the oven on the rack
above the potato wedges 10 minutes before the
potatoes have finished cooking. Sprinkle the fish
with the grated parmesan and serve hot with the
potato wedges.

• Per serving: 359 calories, protein 34g, carbohydrate 34g, fat
11g, saturated fat 2g, fiber 4g, added sugar none, salt 0.43g

Use your microwave to speed up
cooking the baked potatoes.

Smoked Haddock Bake

2 large baking potatoes
8oz fresh baby spinach leaves
4 × 6oz skinless smoked fish fillets
4 tbsp half-and-half
2oz extra sharp cheddar
cheese, grated

Takes 45 minutes • Serves 4

1 Pierce the potatoes all over with a sharp knife.
Microwave on High for 16 minutes. Let stand for 3
minutes, then slice thickly.
2 Scatter the fresh spinach into a large
microwaveable dish and arrange the potatoes on
top. Place the fish on the top of the potatoes. Drop
on spoonfuls of half-and-half and sprinkle with
cheese.
3 Cover with plastic wrap and pierce several times.
Microwave on High for 8 minutes. Let stand for 2
minutes. Remove the plastic wrap. Broil under a
preheated broiler for 3 minutes and serve
immediately.

• Per serving: 334 calories, protein 41g, carbohydrate 23g, fat
9g, saturated fat 9g, fiber 3g, added sugar none, salt 3.86g

Cooked peas add extra color and
flavor to these simple fishcakes.

Smoked Fishcakes

1lb peeled potatoes,
cut into chunks
2 eggs
8oz skinless smoked fish fillets
4 tbsp milk
1oz butter
salt & pepper to taste
6oz frozen peas, thawed
4oz white breadcrumbs
2 tbsp vegetable oil
salad, to serve

Takes 50 minutes • Serves 2

1 Preheat the oven to 400°C. Boil the potatoes and
eggs in salted water for 10–12 minutes. Meanwhile
put the fish, milk and butter in a pan, season with
salt and pepper, cover and simmer for 4–5 minutes.
Strain and reserve the liquid. Flake the fish.
2 Drain the potatoes and eggs. Shell the eggs and
mash them with the potatoes. Add the fish liquid,
season with salt and pepper and stir in the fish and
peas. Shape into six cakes. Press into the breadcrumbs, coating evenly.
3 Pour the oil into a roasting pan. Heat for 5
minutes in the oven. Add the fishcakes, coat in the
oil and cook for 25–30 minutes, turning halfway
through. Serve with salad.

• Per serving: 252 calories, protein 15g, carbohydrate 27g, fat
10g, saturated fat 3g, fiber 3g, added sugar none, salt 1.22g

Salmon takes on the strong flavors
of Chinese cooking very well.

Soy Salmon with Sesame Stir Fry

4 salmon fillets, about 4oz each
3 tbsp soy sauce
2 tbsp honey
finely grated zest and
juice of 1 lemon
2 garlic cloves, thinly sliced
1in piece fresh ginger,
finely grated
8 scallions, finely shredded

FOR THE STIR FRY
1 tsp sesame oil
4oz snow peas
2 medium carrots,
cut into matchsticks
4oz baby corn, halved
2 zucchini, cut into matchsticks

Takes 30 minutes, plus marinating • Serves 4

1 Put the salmon in a shallow dish. Heat the soy sauce, honey, lemon zest and juice, garlic and ginger in a small saucepan with 1 tablespoon of water for 4 minutes. Pour over the salmon and scatter on most of the scallions. Leave to marinate in the refrigerator for at least 30 minutes.

2 Heat the broiler or a griddle pan. Remove the salmon, reserving the marinade. Broil or grill the salmon for 8 minutes, turning once, until tender and golden.

3 Meanwhile, heat a wok or large frying pan to really hot and add the sesame oil. Add the snow peas, carrots and corn, and stir fry for 2 minutes. Add the zucchini and stir fry for 2 minutes. Add the reserved marinade and cook for 2–3 minutes. Serve with the salmon and remaining scallions.

• Per serving: 280 calories, protein 23g, carbohydrate 18g, fat 12g, saturated fat 2.5g, fiber 3g, added sugar none, salt 2.6g

This is a really simple dish that's delicious
served with fried rice or noodles.

Lemon-fried Mackerel

2 lemons
4 ×10oz small whole mackerel or
4 × 5oz other fish fillets
salt & pepper to taste
1 tbsp vegetable oil
3 tbsp soy sauce
1 sugar cube, or 1 tsp sugar
stir-fried rice or noodles, to serve

Takes 25 minutes • Serves 4

1 Thinly slice one of the lemons. Season the fish with salt and pepper, then place the lemon slices down the length of each fish piece. Tie the lemon in place with string.

2 Heat the oil in a large frying pan and cook the fish, lemon-side down, for 3–4 minutes until well browned. Turn and cook the other side for 3 minutes.

3 Add the soy sauce, 4 tablespoons of water and the sugar to the pan. Squeeze in the juice of the remaining lemon and simmer for 2–3 minutes until the fish is cooked through. Serve on a bed of rice or noodles, spooning over the pan juices.

• Per serving: 163 calories, protein 28g, carbohydrate 4g, fat 4g, saturated fat 1g, fiber none, added sugar 1.5g, salt 2.27g

Cheap cans of tomatoes are often a false economy.
Better to go for a good-quality can and keep the flavor fresh.

Shrimp with Tomato and Feta Cheese

3 tbsp olive oil
2 onions, finely chopped
2 × 15oz cans chopped tomatoes
in rich tomato sauce
pinch of sugar
12oz large peeled shrimp,
thawed if frozen
salt & pepper to taste
4oz feta cheese
3 tbsp chopped fresh parsley
rice or pasta, to serve

Takes 20 minutes • Serves 4

1 Heat 3 tablespoons of olive oil in a pan, add the onions and saute gently for about 7 minutes, until softened and light brown. Add the tomatoes and a pinch of sugar and simmer for 5 minutes.

2 Throw in the shrimp, season with salt and pepper and cook gently for 5 minutes until the shrimp are hot all the way through.

3 Serve spooned over rice or pasta. Crumble the feta on top and sprinkle with chopped parsley.

• Per serving: 186 calories, protein 22g, carbohydrate 11g, fat 6g, saturated fat 3g, fiber 3g, added sugar trace, salt 1.54g

With a bag of mixed seafood in the freezer,
you can make a speedy version of a classic dish.

Quick Seafood Paella

1 tbsp sunflower oil
1 onion, finely chopped
1 red pepper, seeded and sliced
2 garlic cloves, finely chopped
8oz can chopped tomatoes
1 tsp turmeric
10oz long-grain rice
4½ cups vegetable stock
16oz bag frozen mixed seafood
(shrimp, mussels, squid,
clams), thawed
6oz green beans, halved
a handful of chopped fresh parsley
salt & pepper to taste
1 lemon, cut into wedges

Takes 30 minutes • Serves 4

1 Heat the oil in a large pan and cook the onion and pepper for 5 minutes until softened but not brown. Stir in the garlic, tomatoes and turmeric and cook for 1 minute more, stirring occasionally.

2 Add the rice and cook for 1 minute, stirring to coat the grains. Pour in the stock, stir well and bring to a boil, then simmer uncovered for 8 minutes, stirring occasionally, until the rice is almost cooked and most of the stock has been absorbed.

3 Add the seafood and beans and cook 3–4 minutes more. Stir in the parsley and season with salt and pepper. Serve straight from the pan with lemon wedges.

• Per serving: 463 calories, protein 32g, carbohydrate 75g, fat 6g, saturated fat 1g, fiber 3g, added sugar none, salt 1.91g

Potatoes and canned beans make this simple supper a filling meal.
Serve with a leafy green salad.

Vegetable and Bean Bake

1 tbsp sunflower oil
2 large onions, thinly sliced
2 garlic cloves, crushed
1 tsp paprika
2 tbsp tomato paste
15oz can cannellini beans,
drained and rinsed
2 tbsp fresh chopped parsley
2 large baking potatoes,
peeled and sliced
1 large zucchini, sliced diagonally
4 ripe tomatoes, sliced
½ cup vegetable stock
1oz grated parmesan cheese

Takes 1½ hours • Serves 4

1 Preheat the oven to 425°F. Heat the oil in a pan. Gently saute the onion and garlic for 10 minutes. Stir occasionally. Add the paprika and cook for 1 minute. Add the tomato paste, beans and parsley. Pour into shallow, ovenproof dish.

2 Parboil the potatoes in lightly salted boiling water for 5 minutes. Drain and spread over the beans. Top with the zucchini and tomatoes.

3 Pour in the stock. Bake for 35 minutes, until tender. Sprinkle with cheese and cook 10 minutes more, until golden.

• Per serving: 304 calories, protein 14g, carbohydrate 50g, fat 7g, saturated fat 2g, fiber 8g, added sugar none, salt 0.57g

A light and colorful warm salad, using
couscous instead of rice or pasta.

Charbroiled Peppers with Couscous

2oz couscous
2 tbsp golden raisins
1 red pepper and ½ yellow
or orange pepper,
seeded and quartered
½ lemon, cut into wedges
1 tsp olive oil
2 tbsp chopped fresh parsley
or cilantro (coriander)
salt & pepper to taste

Takes 10 minutes • Serves 1

1 Put the couscous and raisins in a bowl, add ½
cup boiling water and leave for 5 minutes, until the
water is absorbed. Preheat the broiler.
2 Put the peppers, skin-side up, on the broiler pan
with the lemon wedges, brush with oil and broil for 5
minutes, until the pepper skins are blackened (leave
the skins on for a smoky flavor). Stir the parsley into
the couscous and season with salt and pepper.
3 Spoon the couscous on to a plate, top with the
peppers and squeeze the juice from the broiled
lemon on top. Serve immediately.

• Per serving: 326 calories, protein 7g, carbohydrate 63g, fat
7g, saturated fat 1g, fiber 5g, added sugar none, salt 0.05g

Choose the brown-skinned sweet potatoes
with attractive orange flesh.

Sweet Potato and Cauliflower Curry

1 tbsp vegetable oil
1 onion, chopped
1 garlic clove, crushed
2 tbsp medium hot curry powder
4 tsp all-purpose flour
12oz orange-fleshed sweet
potatoes (brown-skinned),
cut into cubes
12oz cauliflower florets
3 cups vegetable stock
4oz green beans, trimmed
1 tsp garam masala spice mix
naan bread and lime wedges,
to serve

Takes 35 minutes • Serves 4

1 Heat the oil in a large pan and saute the onion for
2–3 minutes, stirring occasionally, until softened. Stir
in the garlic, curry powder and flour and cook for a
minute more.
2 Add the sweet potatoes to the pan, along with the
cauliflower and stock. Bring to a boil and simmer for
10–15 minutes until the potatoes are almost tender.
3 Stir in the green beans and garam masala and
cook for 3 minutes. Serve with warm naan bread
and wedges of lime.

• Per serving: 257 calories, protein 9g, carbohydrate 44g, fat
6g, saturated fat 1g, fiber 6g, added sugar none, salt 0.81g

Thai curries are often thinner and hotter than
Indian curries, with fantastic, vivid flavors.

Thai Red Vegetable Curry

1 tbsp vegetable oil
1 large onion, diced
1lb 2oz sweet potatoes, cubed
10oz squash or zucchini, cubed
9oz green beans
2 tomatoes, diced
2 × 15oz cans coconut milk
2 tsp Thai red curry paste
juice of 1 large lime
2 tbsp soy sauce
a handful of fresh basil or
cilantro (coriander)
salt & pepper to taste
boiled rice, to serve

Takes 35 minutes • Serves 6

1 Heat the oil in a large pan and cook the onion,
sweet potato and squash for 5 minutes until it is
beginning to soften. Cut the beans into 2-inch
lengths, then add them and the tomatoes and cook
2–3 minutes more, until the tomatoes begin to soften.

2 Add the coconut milk and curry paste and bring
to a boil. Cook the mixture for 10–12 minutes until
the vegetables are tender.

Add the lime juice, soy sauce and fresh basil or
coriander; check the seasoning. Serve with boiled
rice.

• Per serving: 170 calories, protein 4g, carbohydrate 34g, fat
3g, saturated fat trace, fiber 5g, added sugar trace, salt 1.44g

This dish is ideal as a starter, but could also be served as an energy-rich snack. It's just as delicious served hot or cold.

Stuffed Peppers

3 small baking potatoes, peeled and cut into thin slices
8 oz pimientos, drained
1 red chili, seeded and finely chopped
1oz pine nuts, toasted
2 garlic cloves, crushed
4 tbsp sundried tomato paste
4oz brown breadcrumbs
2 large red and 2 large yellow peppers, seeded and halved
a handful of fresh basil leaves
2 tbsp rosemary-infused olive oil
salt & pepper to taste
crusty bread, to serve

Takes 1 hour • Serves 8 (as a starter)

1 Preheat the oven to 400°F. Cook the potatoes in lightly salted boiling water for 8 minutes. Drain and set aside. Place the pimientos, chili, pine nuts, garlic, sundried tomato paste and breadcrumbs in a food processor and process to form a coarse paste.
2 Place the pepper halves, skin-side down, in a large roasting pan. Sandwich the potato slices with the pimiento paste and basil leaves and arrange, on their sides, in the pepper halves. Drizzle with the rosemary-infused oil and season with salt and pepper.
3 Bake for 30 minutes, until the peppers are cooked and the potatoes are tender. Serve immediately with crusty bread.

• Per serving: 173 calories, protein 4g, carbohydrate 24g, fat 7g, saturated fat 1g, fiber 3g, added sugar none, salt 0.32g

If you can't find butternut squash, large acorn squash will do.
Or serve the sauce with baked potatoes.

Squash with Tomatoes and Chickpeas

2 medium butternut squash,
about 1lb 9oz each, halved
lengthwise and seeded
1 tbsp olive oil
salt & pepper to taste
1 tbsp balsamic vinegar
1 onion, roughly chopped
4 garlic cloves, peeled and very
thinly sliced
15oz can plum tomatoes
15oz can chickpeas, drained
and rinsed
1 cup vegetable stock
2 tbsp tomato paste
1 tsp fine sugar
a large handful of baby
spinach leaves

Takes 1 hour 20 minutes • Serves 4

1 Preheat the oven to 400°F. Arrange the squash cut side up in a large non-stick roasting pan. Brush with the oil and season generously with salt and pepper. Drizzle with the balsamic vinegar and roast for 45 minutes until just tender.
2 Meanwhile, put the onion, garlic, tomatoes, chickpeas, stock, tomato paste and sugar into a large saucepan. Bring to a boil, break up the tomatoes slightly and simmer for 25 minutes, stirring occasionally, until thickened.
3 Season with salt and pepper to taste. Stir in the spinach and cook until just wilted. Serve the butternut squash with the sauce spooned on top.

• Per serving: 239 calories, protein 10g, carbohydrate 41g, fat 5g, saturated fat none, fiber 8g, added sugar 2g, salt 0.78g

The grated raw beets soften during heating and gives the rice pretty flecks of pink.

Risotto with Beets and Greens

1oz butter
1 onion, chopped
10oz arborio rice
½ cup dry white wine
3 cups vegetable stock
2oz freshly grated parmesan cheese
salt & pepper to taste
5oz mixed grated beets and arugula or baby spinach

Takes 30 minutes • Serves 4

1 Melt half the butter in a pot with a cover. Stir in the onion and cook for 5 minutes until softened but not brown. Add the rice and cook for 3 minutes, stirring to coat the grains. Pour in the wine and boil gently. Stir in the stock and return to a boil. Cover the pot and simmer, without stirring, for 12–15 minutes, until the rice is just tender.
2 Remove from the heat, stir in the parmesan cheese and remaining butter and season with salt and pepper. Add the beets and greens and stir gently until the leaves are wilted; take care not to over-mix or the rice will turn too pink.
3 Divide among warm serving plates and serve sprinkled with freshly ground black pepper.

• Per serving: 398 calories, protein 13g, carbohydrate 62g, fat 10g, saturated fat 6g, fiber 2g, added sugar none, salt 1.23g

The Italians serve soft polenta to soak up delicious sauces.
Here it is used to complement Asian flavors.

Soft Polenta with Bok Choy

5 cups vegetable stock
9oz quick-cook polenta
1 tbsp Thai seven-spice paste
salt & pepper to taste
1 tbsp chili sauce
1 tbsp soy sauce
1 tsp crushed garlic
1 tsp crushed fresh ginger
1 tbsp sesame oil
1 red chili, seeded and thinly sliced
5oz shiitake mushrooms, halved
4 heads bok choy,
halved lengthwise

Takes 25 minutes • Serves 4

1 Pour the stock into a large pot and bring to a rolling boil. Shower in the polenta, stirring constantly. Stir in the Thai paste and simmer gently for 4–5 minutes, stirring. Season with salt and pepper.
2 Mix the chili sauce, soy sauce, garlic, ginger and 2 tablespoons of water together. Heat the sesame oil in a wok and stir fry the chili and mushrooms for 1 minute. Add the bok choy and 4 tablespoons of water and stir fry until the water has evaporated. Add the soy sauce mix and bring to a boil.
3 Divide the polenta between shallow serving bowls and top with the vegetables and dressing. Serve immediately.

• Per serving: 272 calories, protein 9g, carbohydrate 48g, fat 6g, saturated fat 1g, fiber 2g, added sugar none, salt 1.82g

When gnocchi is cooked, it rises to the surface. Vary the recipe by adding peas, beans or anything that strikes your fancy.

Gnocchi Gratin

1 red pepper, seeded and quartered
15oz fresh potato gnocchi
4oz fat-free garlic and herb soft cheese
2½fl oz dry white wine
a large pinch of freshly grated nutmeg
salt & pepper to taste
3oz baby spinach leaves
8 large basil leaves, roughly torn
garlic bread, to serve

Takes 20 minutes • Serves 2

1 Preheat the grill. Broil the pepper quarters, skin-side up, for 7–8 minutes until charred. Place in a plastic bag, seal and let stand 5 minutes to loosen the skins.

2 Bring a large pot of water to a boil and cook the gnocchi according to the package instructions, until they rise to the surface. Meanwhile, in a separate pan warm the soft cheese, wine and nutmeg until melted and hot. Season with salt and pepper.

3 Remove the skin from the peppers and cut the flesh into strips. Toss with the gnocchi, spinach and basil, then pour the melted cheese sauce on top. Serve immediately with garlic bread.

• Per serving: 470 calories, protein 19g, carbohydrate 81g, fat 7g, saturated fat 4g, fiber 6g, added sugar none, salt 0.97g

A veggie version of the traditional Spanish rice dish. Smoked paprika adds extra flavor, but ordinary paprika works too.

Vegetable Paella

2 tbsp olive oil
1 onion, finely chopped
1 garlic clove, crushed
1 red pepper, seeded and finely chopped
1 green pepper, seeded and finely chopped
4oz mushrooms, sliced
8oz long-grain rice
3 cups vegetable stock
½ tsp smoked or ordinary paprika
a large pinch of saffron threads
3oz frozen peas
salt & pepper to taste
2 tomatoes, seeded and finely diced
2 tbsp chopped flatleaf parsley
green salad, to serve

Takes 35 minutes • Serves 4

1 Heat the oil in a frying pan and saute the onion for 2–3 minutes, stirring occasionally, until softened. Add the garlic, red and green peppers and mushrooms and cook for 2–3 minutes more, stirring occasionally.

2 Stir in the rice and saute for 1 minute. Stir in the stock, paprika and saffron. Bring to a boil and simmer for 10–12 minutes, stirring occasionally, until the rice is just tender (add more water if necessary). Stir in the peas and cook 2–3 minutes more. Season with salt and pepper to taste.

3 Spoon the paella on to serving plates and sprinkle the tomato and parsley on top. Serve immediately with a green salad.

• Per serving: 324 calories, protein 7g, carbohydrate 58g, fat 9g, saturated fat 1g, fiber 4g, added sugar none, salt 0.06g

The dimpled apricots look charming left whole, but you can halve them and remove the pits before poaching, if you prefer.

Summery Provençal Apricots

1 bottle dry, fruity rosé wine
6oz fine light brown sugar
1 vanilla bean, split open lengthwise
with a sharp knife, then cut in
quarters (keep the seeds inside)
1lb 9oz ripe fresh apricots
vanilla ice cream, to serve

Takes 40 minutes • Serves 4

1 Pour the wine into a saucepan, add the sugar and then stir in the pieces of vanilla. Stir over a low heat until the sugar has dissolved.

2 Add the apricots. Cover and gently poach until just softened – about 15–20 minutes for whole fruit and 10–15 minutes for halves.

3 Lift the apricots out with a slotted spoon and put them in a bowl. Boil the liquid hard for 8–10 minutes to make a thin syrup. Pour over the apricots and leave to cool. Serve warm or cold, with a piece of vanilla bean to decorate and a scoop of vanilla ice cream.

• Per serving: 356 calories, protein 2g, carbohydrate 62g, fat none, saturated fat 3g, fiber 3g, added sugar 46g, salt 0.03g

Choose an orange-fleshed melon for its color and sweet flavor.
If you have time, chill the melon cubes first.

Melon with Hot Redcurrant Sauce

finely grated zest and juice
of 1 orange
2 tbsp redcurrant jelly
1 ripe orange fleshed melon,
such as cantelope
low-fat natural yogurt, to serve

Takes 10 minutes • Serves 4

1 Put the orange zest and juice in a pan with the redcurrant jelly and a splash of water. Heat gently, stirring occasionally, until the jelly has melted to a smooth sauce.

2 Cut the melon into quarters, discarding the seeds and the skin. Cut the flesh into 1-inch cubes and put in a bowl.

3 Pour the hot redcurrant sauce over the melon, stir well and serve with spoonfuls of yogurt.

• Per serving: 66 calories, protein 1g, carbohydrate 16g, fat trace, saturated fat none, fiber 2g, added sugar none, salt 0.04g

A refreshing palate-cleansing sorbet—great after Mexican food. But watch out, because it has a kick of its own!

Tequila Sunrise Sorbet

8oz fine sugar
juice of 2 limes
juice of 2 lemons
juice of 5 oranges
3½ fl oz tequila, plus extra to serve
1 medium egg white
(raw eggs should be avoided by those who are very young, elderly or pregnant)
4 tbsp grenadine
orange and lime wedges, to serve

Takes 10 minutes, plus freezing • Serves 6

1 Put 3½fl oz water in a large pan with the sugar and fruit juices. Cook over a low heat for 3–4 minutes, stirring until the sugar has dissolved. Boil for 1 minute. Cool completely. Stir in the tequila and chill.

2 Whisk the egg white until stiff and fold into the fruit syrup. Pour half the mixture into a freezerproof container and seal. Stir the grenadine into the other half, mix well and pour into another freezerproof container. Seal. Freeze for 2 hours until slushy around the edges. Break up any ice crystals with a fork and freeze 2 hours more, until solid.

3 Remove the sorbets from the freezer 20 minutes before serving. Frost the serving dishes with egg white and sugar. Scoop both sorbets into each dish. Pour a shot of tequila on top and decorate with citrus wedges.

• Per serving: 211 calories, protein 1g, carbohydrate 39g, fat 0.01g, saturated fat none, fiber 0.11g, added sugar 35g, salt 0.03g

Check that the melons are really ripe and
fragrant for the best flavor.

Melon and Ginger Sorbet

3lb 5oz honeydew, halved
and seeded
3oz fine sugar
4 pieces candied ginger in syrup,
drained and chopped
1 medium egg white
(raw eggs should be
avoided by those who are very
young, elderly or pregnant)

Takes 15 minutes, plus freezing • Serves 4

1 Scoop out the flesh from the melons and place in a food processor with the sugar. Process until smooth, then stir in the ginger and transfer to a shallow freezerproof dish. Freeze for 2 hours until mushy.

2 Whisk the egg white until just stiff but not dry. Remove the iced melon from the freezer and mash with a fork, then stir in the egg white.

3 Return to the freezer for 2 hours more, until frozen. Serve decorated with extra ginger, if you like.

• Per serving: 173 calories, protein 3g, carbohydrate 42g, fat 0.4g, saturated fat 0.01g, fiber 2g, added sugar 21g, salt 0.33g

Leave the brûlée topping until the last minute,
because it slowly softens as it stands.

Strawberry Yogurt Brûlée

1lb 2oz strawberries
juice of 1 orange
16oz natural yogurt
4oz fine sugar

Takes 30 minutes, plus chilling • Serves 6

1 Slice the strawberries and divide among six serving dishes or glasses. Sprinkle on the orange juice, then spoon the yogurt on top. Chill until ready to serve.

2 Put the sugar in a small pan with 2 tablespoons of cold water. Heat gently, stirring to dissolve the sugar, then increase the heat and stop stirring. Boil the mixture carefully until it turns a light caramel color, then remove from the heat and plunge the base of the pan into a sink filled with cold water to stop it cooking further.

3 When the bubbles have subsided, carefully pour a little syrup over each dessert. Leave for 10 minutes before serving, or chill for up to an hour.

• Per serving: 202 calories, protein 7g, carbohydrate 43g, fat 1g, saturated fat 1g, fiber 1g, added sugar 26g, salt 0.26g

For a special occasion, substitute half a cup of red wine for half the apple juice .

Poached Pears with Blackberries

4 medium pears
zest of 1 lemon (remove with a potato peeler)
1 tbsp lemon juice
9oz blackberries
1 cup unsweetened apple juice
2oz fine light brown sugar
8 tbsp fat-free mild yogurt

Takes 40 minutes • Serves 4

1 Peel the pears but don't remove their stems. Place them in a saucepan with the lemon zest and juice, half the blackberries, the apple juice and the sugar. Heat until simmering, then cover and cook gently for 20–25 minutes until the pears are tender, turning them once.

2 Remove the pears from the liquid and cool for a few minutes. Halve each, core with a teaspoon or a melon baller, and transfer to four dishes.

3 Strain the liquid through a sieve into a pan. Add the remaining blackberries and warm gently. Serve the pears and blackberries with the yogurt.

• Per serving: 180 calories, protein 5g, carbohydrate 41g, fat 0g, saturated fat 0g, fiber 5g, added sugar 13g, salt trace

The apricots can be cooked up to two days ahead and stored in the refrigerator. Try serving this dish for breakfast.

Banana and Apricot Compote

9oz dried apricots
7fl oz apple juice
2 bananas, peeled and sliced
4 passion fruit (or a pint of
of raspberries)
2 tbsp toasted flaked almonds
yogurt or sour cream and plain
wafer cookies, to serve

Takes 30 minutes, plus cooling • Serves 4

1 Put the apricots, apple juice and 7fl oz water in a pot. Bring to a boil, cover and simmer for 20 minutes.

2 Remove from the heat and leave to cool. You can make this dish in advance to this stage.

3 Put the cooled apricots in a bowl and stir in the banana. Mix in the flesh from the passion fruit. Sprinkle the almonds over the fruit and serve with yogurt and cookies.

• Per serving: 341 calories, protein 7g, carbohydrate 71g, fat 5g, saturated fat trace, fiber 8g, added sugar none, salt 0.13g

Mincemeat is actually a sweet mixture of raisins, candied citrus peel, nuts and other ingredients. Look for it in jars, or try sweet chutney.

Marzipan and Mincemeat Apples

2 medium Granny Smith apples
3oz marzipan, chopped
8 tbsp mincemeat
finely grated zest and juice of 1 small lemon
natural yogurt, to serve

Takes 25 minutes • Serves 4

1 Cut the apples in half widthwise. Remove and discard the cores, then set the apples in a microwave-proof dish, cut side up. Mix the marzipan with the mincemeat and lemon zest. Spoon into the center of the apples and spoon on the lemon juice.
2 Cover the dish with plastic wrap, pierce several times and microwave on High for 4½ minutes. If you don't have a turntable and the apples are not cooking evenly, turn the dish halfway through.
3 Remove the plastic wrap and let stand for 5 minutes before serving with natural yogurt.

• Per serving: 200 calories, protein 2g, carbohydrate 41g, fat 4g, saturated fat 1g, fiber 2g, added sugar 24g, salt trace

This is an easy, no-fuss cherry and lemon
version of the classic French recipe.

Cheat's Clafoutis

1lb cherries, pitted
2 tbsp cherry, plum or apricot jam
finely grated zest and juice
of 1 lemon
2oz all-purpose flour
3 eggs
16fl oz skim milk
½ tsp ground cinnamon
3 tbsp golden fine sugar
confectioner's sugar, to dust

Takes 50 minutes • Serves 2–3

1 Preheat the oven to 375°F. Lightly oil a shallow
baking dish. Gently heat the cherries and jam in a
large saucepan, stirring until the jam melts over the
cherries. Put them in the baking dish and sprinkle
with the lemon zest and juice.
2 Process the flour, eggs, milk, cinnamon and sugar
in a food processor for 30 seconds, until smooth.
Pour over the cherries.
3 Put the dish on a baking tray and bake for
25–30 minutes or until the custard is set and the
jam is beginning to bubble through. Dust with
confectioner's sugar and serve hot.

• Per serving: 532 calories, protein 23g, carbohydrate 92g, fat
11g, saturated fat 3g, fiber 2g, added sugar 38g, salt 0.66g

Date purée replaces the fat in this
tempting recipe, with nothing lost.

Guilt-free Sticky Toffee Cakes

6oz pitted dried dates
¼ pint maple syrup
1 tbsp vanilla extract
2 eggs, separated
3oz self-rising flour
fat-free mild yogurt and extra maple
syrup, to serve (optional)

Takes 1½ hours • Serves 4

1 Preheat the oven to 350°F. Simmer the dates in
6fl oz water for 5 minutes. Put in a food processor,
add 6 tablespoons of maple syrup and the vanilla,
and blend until smooth. Transfer to a bowl and mix
in the egg yolks, followed by the flour.
2 Whisk the egg whites until stiff and fold into the
date mixture. Put 1 tablespoon of maple syrup into
each of four 7fl oz custard cups. Add the mixture.
Cover each tightly with foil, stand in an ovenproof
dish and pour in hot water to halfway up the sides of
the molds. Cook for 1 hour, until a toothpick inserted
into the centre comes out clean.
3 Uncover, run a knife around the edges, and invert
onto plates. Drizzle the yogurt and maple syrup on
top to serve.

• Per serving: 339 calories, protein 7g, carbohydrate 73g, fat
4g, saturated fat 1g, fiber 2g, added sugar 25g, salt 0.33g

Index

Picture credits and recipe credits

BBC Worldwide would like to thank the following for providing photographs. While every effort has been made to trace and acknowledge all photographers, we would like to apologize for are any errors or omissions.

Chris Alack p53, p59, p111; Iain Bagwell p73, p141, p161, p203; Clive Bozzard-Hill p175; Jean Cazals p15, p37; Ken Field p45, p95, p123, p153, p199; Hulton Archive p55; David Jordan p181, p189; Dave King p117, p119, p125, p163; Richard Kolker p191; Steve Lee p79; David Munns p13, p21, p35, p39, p81, p107, p155, p159; Myles New p43, p89, p139, p211; Nick Pope p33; Bill Reavell p177; Simon Smith p185; Roger Stowell p17, p19, p23, p27, p31, p41, p47, p63, p65, p77, p83, p87, p91, p93, p99, p101, p105, p109, p115, p121, p131, p143, p149, p151, p171, p183, p193, p195, p201, p207; Martin Thompson p11, p57, p69; Martin Thompson and Philip Webb p113; Trevor Vaughan p187; Simon Walton p51, p61, p75, p85, p133, p135, p147, p165, p209; Philip Webb p157; Simon Wheeler p67, p71, p97, p103, p127, p137, p145, p169; Jonathan Whitaker p29, p129, p173; Frank Wieder p197; Geoff Wilkinson p167, p179, p205; BBC Worldwide p25, p49

All the recipes in this book have been created by the editorial teams on *BBC Good Food Magazine* and *BBC Vegetarian Good Food Magazine*.

Angela Boggiano, Lorna Brash, Sara Buenfeld, Mary Cadogan, Gilly Cubitt, Barney Desmazery, Joanna Farrow, Rebecca Ford, Silvana Franco, Catherine Hill, Jane Lawrie, Clare Lewis, Sara Lewis, Liz Martin, Kate Moseley, Orlando Murrin, Vicky Musselman, Angela Nilsen, Justine Pattison, Jenny White and Jeni Wright.